BOARDROOM DANCING

March 2025

Emma

Congratulations on your promotion!

I eagerly anticipate your presence in the Boardrooms of South Africa & beyond.

Rise up, make an impact and embrace all of who you are ♡

Love
Sash &
Aunty Ann
♡x♡x

BOARDROOM DANCING

Transformation stories
from a corporate activist

Nolitha Fakude

MACMILLAN

First published in 2019
by Pan Macmillan South Africa
Private Bag X19
Northlands
2116
Johannesburg
South Africa

www.panmacmillan.co.za

ISBN 978-1-77010-684-0
E-ISBN 978-1-77010-685-7

© Nolitha Fakude 2019

All rights reserved. No part of this publication may be reproduced, stored in or introduced into a retrieval system, or transmitted, in any form, or by any means (electronic, mechanical, photocopying, recording or otherwise), without the prior written permission of the publisher. Any person who does any unauthorised act in relation to this publication may be liable to criminal prosecution and civil claims for damages.

Every attempt has been made to ensure the accuracy of the details, facts, names, places and events mentioned in these pages, but the publisher and author welcome any feedback, comments and/or corrections.

Editing by Alison Lowry
Proofreading by Kelly Norwood-Young
Design and typesetting by Triple M Design, Johannesburg
Cover design by Hybrid Creative
Cover photograph courtesy of Sasol

Printed by **novus print**, a division of Novus Holdings

Dedicated to the memory of my Grand Mother –
Vuyelwa Elizabeth Nosizwe 'Mangangenkomo' Njoli –
Imazi etsala nenkabi.
You were and still are my SOURCE. Your footprints are deep in my heart!

To my son Phila – you are my everyday inspiration.
I'm so proud of the man you have become.

Contents

Definitions xiii
Foreword *by Dr Phumzile Mlambo-Ngcuka* xvii

Prelude 1
Prologue 7

PART 1: EARLY YEARS

1 Growing up in a matriarchy 13
    Ngqika Store 18
    Special treatment 21

2 Bethel College 26
    Good works 29
    A cruel system 32

3 Finding my freedom 35
    Getting serious 37
    In search of life experience 41

PART 2: STEPPING OUT

4 Liberations 45
    'The University of Retail' 48
    Small steps towards change 50
    Learning to lead 58

5 Embracing democracy 63
    When magic showed its face 66
    My Cape Town 71

6 Earning a place at the table 73
    'Suitably qualified' 74
    The value of a mentor 80
    Network exposure 83
    National debates 89

PART 3: A NATIONAL STAGE

7 Synergistic symphonies: The power of collaborations 99
    Managing director 101
    Sector charters 103
    Compromise and negotiation 106
    Culture change 108
    One business voice 110

8 (Redefining) a woman's place 113
    A breakthrough for the gender agenda 115
    The power of influence 118
    Skills development and training 120
    Social impact agenda 122

9 Another kind of integration 126
    Business transformation 127

The value of the insider-outsider 129
The stretch assignment 132
Personal transformations 133

10 Preparing to fly 138
Legacies 142

PART 4: GLOBAL TRANSFORMATIONS

11 Awakening a South African giant 149
Interventions 152
Uncomfortable conversations 157
Shifting culture 159
A higher purpose 163

12 Thinking globally, acting locally 166
Milestones 170
Personal success 176

13 Extending my reach 177
Getting noticed 180
Change and evolution 182
False dichotomies 183
The next challenge 188
A tribute by Imogen Mkhize 189

PART 5: THE JOURNEY AHEAD

14 Reigniting the gender agenda 195
The 'firstborn' generation: A responsibility and a privilege 196
Equal opportunity 199
Sharing the load 203
Aligning the head and heart 205

15 We need to talk 207
    My soapbox manifesto 210
    How do we get there: Rules of engagement 212

Appendix: Correspondence close to my heart 216
Abbreviations 221
Notes 225
Acknowledgements 227
Selected references and suggested reading 229

Definitions

Because these key terms have very specific meanings in the South African context, I have provided the following definitions in order to ensure a common starting point:

Affirmative action (AA), first used as a term in the United States (US), is defined as 'an action that favours those who tend to suffer from discrimination, or positive discrimination'. It resulted in policies of affirmative action being applied in the US in the 1960s. In South Africa it was applied in the 1940s specifically to benefit white Afrikaners and later, in the 1980s, to benefit black South Africans (those classified African, Indian and coloured). After 1994, a policy of Employment Equity (EE) was implemented in South Africa through the Employment Equity Act No. 55 of 1998, with the purpose of 'hiring policies' encouraging fair representation of groups such as black people, women, people living with disabilities and other minority groups that were previously discriminated against by the laws of South Africa and were thus disadvantaged, specifically economically.

Bantu education
H.F. Verwoerd, the architect of apartheid, is infamously quoted as saying, in the 1950s: *'There is no place for [the Bantu] in the European community above*

the level of certain forms of labour ... What is the use of teaching the Bantu child mathematics when it cannot use it in practice? That is quite absurd. Education must train people in accordance with their opportunities in life, according to the sphere in which they live.' It is in this context – of an intentionally inferior education for black people so as to limit their opportunities and expectations and continue to direct them to lower grades of employment – that the term 'Bantu education' is referred to in this book.

Black Economic Empowerment (BEE), as defined on Wikipedia, is 'a racially selective programme launched by the South African government to redress the inequalities of apartheid by giving Black (African, Coloureds and Indians) South African citizens economic privileges that are not available to Whites.' In the case of South Africa, we are talking about 'legitimate differentiation' as espoused by the United Nations Covenant under Convention 84 (elimination of all forms of racial discrimination). In South Africa, therefore, employment equity and black economic empowerment are a human rights issue first and foremost. Section Nine of the South African Constitution gives citizens the right to equality; furthermore, it 'allows for affirmative action to redress past unfair discrimination'. The South African government has put in place all these interventions to create the so-called level playing field for black South Africans who were historically disadvantaged by the practices of economic exclusion of the apartheid government. The role of both the private and public sectors in levelling this playing field is critical. It has become even more urgent to address this seeing that it is 25 years since we attained our democracy. Failure to effectively level this playing field will mean that South Africa's black economic empowerment as envisaged in the Constitution will be incomplete.

Coloured person
In South Africa the term 'coloured' has been widely used to describe mixed-race people, whose ancestry often includes a mix of Khoi-San, black African, European and possibly Malay heritage. In South Africa, coloured people are

a recognised ethnic group with a culture that not only draws from their vast ancestral cultures but also their history in the South African context. It is a term used today by many people who self-identify as coloured and it is by no means laden with the same derogatory sense it carries in the US, although the term is also not without controversy.

Transformation (key phrases: deep change; shifted state of being/doing) is the process of deep change that takes place within an organisation or institution, resulting in significant shifts of being and doing (for example, from one state of cultural practices, behaviours and sometimes business processes to a different and evolved state of being and doing). We change and shift culture as part of the transformation process, resulting in evolved or new ways of doing things. When we transform in an organisation we can never go back to the old behaviours and processes. For a caterpillar to become a butterfly, it must undergo a full metamorphosis. That is true and lasting transformation. To ensure that the deep changes we seek and need for the culture, processes and practices of an organisation are lasting, we require the following interventions:

- a paradigm shift regarding the culture we want to change
- tools to embed the new desired changes (for example, values aligned to support our vision, Employment Equity Act, BBBEE Act)
- a review of the processes and practices based on the desired vision and purpose.

Foreword

The story of Nolitha Fakude is a masterclass in how a young black girl, who grew up under apartheid South Africa and was raised in a small village in the Eastern Cape, stood up for herself, took hold of the opportunities she identified as stepping stones, and became one of our best. Our South African liberation story was meant to give us many more stories like this one. This is a dream we cannot give up on. Nolitha Fakude shows us that such dreams can come true.

The insight Nolitha gives us into her life, from early years learning the basics of business at her single mother's knee in the family's general store to the air-conditioned atmosphere of the boardroom, is an invaluable opportunity for us to learn how success might be achieved.

We learn from this book that while it is not easy for a black woman in South Africa to rise to the top, it is also not impossible. It is hard work, hard fight and it pays to have mentors and promoters as well as to hold on to your truths. I hope many South Africans who doubt themselves or those who sometimes feel discouraged will read this book, gain new energy and stay woke.

Nurtured and supported by her loving family, Nolitha was determined to get a university qualification and setbacks did not stop her from fulfilling this dream. As a young student she chose a balanced life. She pursued her studies and her love of music saw her fight hard to be in the school choir. The balanced life between academics and extra-murals prepared her for a life with multiple high-stakes roles. When she stepped into the corporate space, she focused on being a high performer, continued to fight for her rights and learned to be collegial in a potentially racially polarised work environment.

Nolitha is of the generation of professionals, black and white, who were trailblazers. They gave shape and meaning to Black Economic Empowerment, whether it progressed or stalled. Nolitha's trailblazing spirit was enriched by her leadership position in the Black Management Forum (BMF), a position that came with a need to embrace a political role and to be part of the national discourse on economic transformation.

For all of these roles there were no pioneers to learn from, no playbook or application to turn to for guidance and facilitation. Nolitha's cohort of leaders created the trail. We celebrate all of the milestones and the role played by the BMF in the era of Nolitha. Her move to Sasol and the international arena was another mountain to climb in the transformation journey, but for this girl from the Eastern Cape no mountain was too high. And the journey is not over. Tackling gender inequality needs the lessons and experience gained by these trailblazing leaders. South Africa needs more boardroom dancers like Nolitha Fakude.

Dr Phumzile Mlambo-Ngcuka
Under-Secretary-General of the United Nations and
Executive Director of UN Women
August 2019

Prelude

As much as others were toyi-toying on the streets for our political, social and economic freedom, some of us were toyi-toying inside South Africa's corporate boardrooms for socio-economic empowerment ...

The story of South Africa's freedom since 1994 is nearly always told from the political as well as the social perspective, while the economic empowerment successes and failures are told from a narrowly defined BEE perspective. The story has never been told from an affirmative action and employment equity perspective, through the eyes and lived experiences of one of its most visible beneficiaries, both from a race and gender perspective. I am that beneficiary and this is my story.

It was by sheer coincidence that my career started in June 1990, shortly after Nelson Mandela was released from prison in February that momentous year. That my corporate journey continued through the first 25 years of South Africa's democracy felt relevant and worth exploring further and sharing with others, not only for the invaluable insights I gained along the way, but also in order to document my professional path so far.

I started working when I was eight years old. My father had died and left my 28-year-old mother bereft with grief and with three children to take care of, aged seven, five and three months old. So my mother needed all hands on deck to get life back to normal. Being one of those hands on deck became my routine until I got married.

Forty-three years later it was time to come up for air. I was due for a gap year.

Besides, if I was to be a productive world citizen and a caring member of the human race, I realised that I needed time out to re-energise, and get myself grounded and refocused. I had just turned 51 and I needed time for reflection and planning for the next 50 years, God willing.

From the day people heard that I was leaving Sasol after eleven years, many of them called to find out about my next plans. At the time I had one big master plan: to take a gap year. That's what I told them. However, these people encouraged me to think differently about this gap year, reminding me not to squander the time. I'm truly grateful for their thoughtfulness and encouragement.

'Write a book!' That was what both Onkgopotse 'JJ' Tabane and Muzi Khuzwayo said (independently of each other) without skipping a beat. 'I'll help you get started ...' 'Please call on me, if you need to ...' They each, in their own crazy way, nudged and coached me to get the book ball rolling. (You are true brothers-in-arms – thank you!)

Professor Michael Katz called and got straight to the point: 'Are you okay?' he asked. 'Please come for a cup of tea soon.' Knowing how tough corporate boardrooms are, he wanted to give me a 'safe space' to talk in case I needed that. Fortunately, all I needed at the time was his big warm hug and assurances that I was not mad for wanting a clean break rather than a sabbatical.

Vukile – my cousin from my father's side and our elder in the AmaHegebe and abaThembu clans – insisted on visiting me at home to make sure that I was really okay.

Reuel Khoza was another concerned friend. 'What are you up to?' he asked in his firm big-brother voice. Then, encouragingly: 'If you can, please write your story while you have this break. We need more black business voices out there. We don't write enough.'

Allon Raiz asked me to do a few podcast/videos with him for his TV programme *The Big Small Business*, on leadership, values and mentorship. These sharpened my resolve to write the memoir from that perspective.

PRELUDE

Nene Molefe unstintingly shared with me her tips on getting started.

Hlengani Mathebula, my self-appointed 'bodyguard', especially during the Black Management Forum (BMF) years, was adamant that my BMF journey deserved to be told through my eyes as well.

All of these people, and many others, offered me moral support and gave me the confidence to believe that I had a story to tell. After being on this earth for more than five decades, surely I had earned the right to tell 'Our story' of corporate South Africa's transformation from my perspective, for My story is Our story.

My story is a tale of many shared experiences that so many of us who grew up in South Africa pre-1994 with affirmative action and post-1994 with employment equity know so well. As much as the characters I describe along my journey may be completely different to yours, so, too, might they be familiar, or even shockingly close.

It should come as no surprise that this memoir demonstrates that in my case the 'personal is political', both at home as well as professionally. As I moved between the different boardrooms that I was involved with at the time, the political context was always there. The black economic empowerment and transformation mandate was implicit in everything I (we) did. Against many odds, as black professionals in the 90s and black women professionals in particular, we had everything thrown at us to slow down our career trajectories, from comments about our engagement style (perceived as aggressive and not assertive), to comments about our heavy African accent and including the label of not being 'ready' every time an opportunity for promotion presented itself. It took great tenacity but we thrived and excelled, not least because we knew that anything less would reinforce the negative stereotypes at play at the time.

Embarking on this process of writing down the years has been challenging and the journey a cathartic one. I've had more moments of reflection and understanding of the meaning of why and how certain people came into my life in the last 24 months than I've had in my entire life. As a result, there are probably more books in the proverbial pipeline, and many stories still to be told that I have deliberately not included in this memoir. With some stories, it's a question of timing, while others will forever be buried in my heart and mind and will never see the light of day. During this journey and time of reflection I've laid a lot of ghosts to rest but also woken up a few sleeping dogs.

From when I was a child, I've always believed that I've led a charmed life regardless of what challenges I have faced. Writing this book has confirmed this further for me. As a result, I'm also crystal clear about my purpose in life. I am convinced that kindness in itself is the religion I subscribe to and of which I am an unapologetic disciple. My entire life has been filled with generosity and abundance more than it has been touched by sadness or bitterness, thanks to the many known and unknown people who have been my 'guardian angels'. If I had not written this memoir I might not have had this deep insight, and so I'm grateful to have had this gap year.

Looking at my corporate career so far – and I include my eight-year-old self here – a snapshot takeaway summary might look something like this:

Ngqika Store, my grandmother's and later my mother's general dealer shop – Kwa NoDumo, as the villagers called it – was where my business and leadership skills were nurtured. The seeds and roots of social solidarity and empathy were planted in Kwa NoDumo Cash Store (my anchor).

Woolworths set a firm and solid business foundation ('the University of Retail').

Nedbank became my business school testing ground.

Sasol became my global stage (Mozambique, Uzbekistan, Qatar, China and the US – where we had our secondary listing on the NYSE – were among the many countries in which we operated).

The BMF was my life's 'true north'. My life and my career were enriched by the BMF, for which I will always be grateful.

All the above organisations have strong recognisable brands, good value systems, a culture of high performance, and are seen/perceived to be good corporate citizens within the South African business landscape. That association for me personally has been deliberate and important. A company's reputation is as important as my own reputation!

PRELUDE

Throughout the years, especially during my eleven years at Sasol, I believe that I've always had the best teams for my functions. These women and men, young and old, made me proud to be part of their teams. Extremely competent, competitive and great fun to be with. I spent hours with my teams, often in awe of what each person brought to the table in terms of thought leadership and quality of work. For my part, I was always working hard not to let them down and together we glided through many boardrooms as we strived to deliver our mandate.

In the pages that follow, as I recount my progression through my business life, a strong thread will be discerned – a thread that is held and sustained by women. Throughout my life, women have particularly embraced me in so many ways, women I know and women I don't know: 'nindenze umntu, ngokwenene, umuntu ngumuntu ngabantu'.

The women of the BMF and its sister organisations became the rock that I could stand on. They built a wall of goodwill and love around me and helped to anchor me against storms so big that on my own I would have been buried alive many times over. I stood with them in spirit, whatever platform I was on. Ndiyabulela ...

As women in South Africa, we benefited immensely from Thabo Mbeki's feminist approach during his presidency. Within corporates his policies and personal commitment to gender equity gave us the boost we required. My ascension to the BMF presidency had a lot to do with the tailwinds and sentiments he held regarding the pace or lack of transformation in corporate South Africa, specifically with regard to black people and generally when it came to women. This was how Bheki Sibiya could confidently step up and throw down the gauntlet to the BMF membership as a whole. I remember him saying to me, 'MaNjoli, the gender agenda is an idea whose time has come. The BMF must not be ambivalent about it.'

It has to be said that after President Mbeki, there was no political will from business to drive transformation. The call for 'Radical Economic Transformation' from the political leadership soon paralysed even those who wanted to do something when it became clear that in many instances

PRELUDE

RET was becoming synonymous with corruption. The transformation agenda was being hijacked right in front of our eyes and the voice of black professionals muzzled by the fear of being called 'clever blacks'. For a private sector that in the first instance had had no real appetite for the transformation agenda, this was a convenient hiatus (people would just throw up their hands and roll their eyes). The message and tone from the top was too confusing and ambivalent, especially on the issue of gender equity.

My hope in writing this memoir at this particular juncture in my own life, and in the life of our nation, is that it will invoke in you, the reader, the urge to want to have a much more open and deeper discussion about what our shared future should look like and what the common values of South Africa should be, and how best to move forward as a country towards defining a peaceful co-existence among all South Africans of all races by leveraging the economic transformation framework that exists in South Africa.

If I am able in some small way to play a part in encouraging and guiding that discussion, my gap year will have been fruitful indeed.

Prologue

I stood transfixed on the spot. I focused on the picture hanging in the office of Busi Mavuso – managing director of the Black Management Forum (BMF) – and took a deep breath. Then, channelling my grandmother, Mangangenkomo, I calmly returned to the boardroom. 'Apologies, gentlemen,' I said. 'Where were we?'

Another chapter had just begun.

Half an hour earlier I had been forced to open the BMF meeting of its Council of Elders by apologising upfront for the fact that I had to keep my phone on. I was expecting a call that could not be put off. When my phone rang, I escaped to Busi's office to take it in privacy.

'Good afternoon, Ms Fakude, it's John here. Thanks for taking my call. Did you travel well back to South Africa?' said Sir John Parker, the chairman of the Anglo American plc board.

'Yes, thanks, Sir John. I did. All is well,' I replied, feeling anxious.

'The nominations committee members really enjoyed meeting you last week,' Sir John Parker continued, referring to our meeting the week before in London. 'We are hoping that you will honour us by accepting our invitation to join the Anglo American plc board.'

I took a deep breath, and responded as elegantly as I could.

'Thank you, Sir John, it will be my honour to accept.' As if I would have declined a board seat on one of the London Stock Exchange (LSE) FTSE 100 and the JSE Top 40 Listed companies.

He thanked me and filled me in on the details, which I heard through a surreal fog. 'I wanted to congratulate you personally. Goodbye, Nolitha,' he said, signing off.

It was February 2017, two months into my gap year, for which I had set myself three goals. One was to try to write this memoir. Second, I needed to centre and energise myself by reconnecting with the people I had not had enough time to see for some years due to my hectic work schedule. And third, I wanted to serve as a non-executive director with a portfolio of at least three boards so as to keep my brain stimulated. Included in my board wish-list was the desire to be on an internationally listed entity. Although the plan had been to start looking later in the year within new sectors, opportunities like the Anglo American plc had already started knocking. Sometimes you simply must seize the moment.

I had been a non-executive director from as early as 2000, when I had been invited to join the now defunct Peoples Bank board. Over the years I would have the privilege of serving on various boards of companies in different parts of the private sector: Harmony Gold (mining), Woolworths Holdings (retail), and Datacentrix (ICT). I also got to sit on boards of organisations in other sectors, from education (CHIETA SETA) to sports (AFCON 2013 LOC) to engineering (Bigen Africa), among others. While I had been on JSE- and NYSE-listed companies, I had never served on an LSE-listed company, and my gap year offered this new opportunity. What an education!

◇◇◇◇◇

With each company and organisation comes new language as well as culture. However, as much as the various boards I have been part of had their own distinct look (composition of members) and feel (protocols and behaviours), one thing they all shared was being composed of men and women who were top achievers and subject-matter experts in their respective fields. All these boards were also underpinned by the immense respect that flowed between individuals with great admiration for each other as professionals.

Having said this, as a new director, I have always found that for at least the first year or so, you do a lot of listening, observing and questioning as you try to decipher the dance at play within that particular organisation and boardroom. Initially you may feel slow, even occasionally stumbling. However, in no time you get into the rhythm of things. That is the time to look at things with clear eyes and fresh ears so that you can use your voice with impact. Soon thereafter you become one of them.

The boardroom is an exhilarating space populated mostly by self-actualised people who are at the top of their game. More often than not, the average age on most boards tends to be in the 50s – the point in your life when you can engage with executive management with circumspection and courtesy, while also offering your own inputs with confidence to your peers. Non-executive directorship is a role of questions more than answers: an oversight rather than an operational role. If there's one thing I've learned from all my experience on different boards, it is that your premise should always be, 'I don't know what I don't know about your business, so help me understand …' Which is when the dance begins …

PART 1

◇◇◇◇◇◇◇◇◇◇◇◇◇◇◇

EARLY YEARS

Adapting does not mean you forget.
STEVE BIKO

From *The Testimony of Steve Biko*, edited by Millard W. Arnold

CHAPTER 1

Growing up in a matriarchy

It was a regular evening in early 2004 and I was busy preparing for a meeting the next day, enjoying the second wind I usually get in the stillness that comes after dinner, when my phone rang. It was my Aunt Zet.

'Litha, do you have the TV on?' she said, her voice full of excitement.

'What's this about?' I asked, searching for the remote and switching on the TV.

Images of a down-and-out white man in his early 30s gave way to those of the clapboard façade of my family's general store back in Cenyu, the small village where I grew up in the Eastern Cape. The newscaster's voice explained that the man had shown up at a police station in Mpumulanga province, claiming that a 'coloured' family had kidnapped him, and that he was seeking his white parents.

'It's your child – Ebbie,' Aunt Zet said, as an image of the blue-eyed boy whom we had called 'Happy' filled the screen.

I had no idea how Happy had ended up on TV like this. Shocking as it was, his sad story was all too typical in the way it illustrated the brokenness at the root of our country's history – a profound chasm of structural racism and inequality that I had increasingly focused my professional life on helping to fill.

With a population of about 350, the small village of my youth was the kind of place where everyone knew each other. My family owned the village

PART 1: EARLY YEARS

store where people came to communicate with family members working as migrant labourers elsewhere, and I often helped read and write letters or put through phone calls from the shop's phone. As a result, I often knew more than I should have about people's personal lives and struggles.

A domestic worker in Joburg, Ebbie's mother had brought him to Cenyu when I was about eight. Still a small baby, Ebbie was left with his pensioner grandmother so his mother could return to her job in the city. It soon became obvious that Ebbie was a mixed-race child – the result of an 'illegal union', according to South Africa's anti-miscegenation laws at the time – and as he grew, Ebbie's blue eyes and fair skin made him the target of taunts and bullying.

From my family's shop, which in many ways was a centre of the community, it was not unusual for us to hear Ebbie being teased (the kids in the village calling him '*amper baas*', Afrikaans for 'almost-white boss') or worse. Often we would find him crying after having been beaten by other boys who resented the idea that this child would someday grow into a white man. As his grandmother spent most of her time drinking homebrewed beer, Ebbie not only lacked protection from the bullying, he also was not well looked after.

I was away at boarding school by the time most of this was happening, but I knew my mother gave Ebbie food to eat when he came around, and let him ride with her in the bakkie when she went to run errands in town, as he didn't seem to be in school. Whenever I was home and saw Ebbie hanging around the shop, I would engage with him and look after him, and people used to jokingly refer to him as my child.

During my last year at boarding school when I was seventeen, I was home helping out in the shop when there was a big commotion outside and I heard people screaming, 'Ebbie, Ebbie!'

I found Ebbie outside on the ground, unconscious and foaming at the mouth. Taking him to the hospital, I discovered he had passed out from hunger, and had apparently been eating grass. Although many people in Cenyu could have been called poor, most had vegetable gardens and there was an unspoken rule that as black people we helped one another. But Ebbie was not seen as black.

A couple of months later on the phone with my mom, she informed me that a social worker had taken Ebbie from his grandmother and put him into foster care. His stay at hospital had obviously alerted people to this 'embarrassment' of a 'white' child living in the black village. We later heard that a coloured family in town had adopted him, and figured that was the end of the story.

But now, 20 years later, here was Ebbie on TV, claiming to have been kidnapped. I can only assume that it was the trauma of his childhood that caused him to distort his history and reality so completely. The headlines died as soon as Ebbie got new benefactors in Johannesburg, people who did not think that he was 'just crazy'. Sadly, about ten years later I heard that he had been killed in a shebeen fight.

Despite people teasingly calling him my child, I didn't actually know Ebbie well at all. But the unfairness of his treatment in our community left a mark on me. Growing up in our shop, absorbing people's stories and hardships, I developed empathy and a desire to understand people. I hated knowing that people were treated badly because they were different, and I often thought about all the paths Ebbie's life could have taken had he simply been born with a different colour skin.

The brokenness of the man who started out as a child who had done nothing worse than exist as the wrong colour in the wrong place at the wrong time served as yet another example of the waste and suffering that results from viewing our fellow human beings as others to exclude rather than potential to develop. Over the years, a question that has come to guide my life is how we can move as a society from viewing the differences as a weakness to viewing them as positive in order to benefit everyone.

⚬⚬⚬⚬⚬

I was born on 27 October 1964 to Victor Mthunzi Njoli and Yolisa NoDumo Njoli (née Ntuthu) and raised in Cenyu, one of several villages outside the town of Stutterheim. In those days the town of Stutterheim was 100% white, and black people lived either on the farms around the town or in villages like Cenyu. The Njoli family comes from the AmaHegebe clan of the AbaThembu tribe, and the Ntuthu family is from the AmaBhele clan. Surrounded by the lush green hills of the Eastern Cape, Cenyu sat in the dip of a forested valley, making it perpetually cold and wet when it rained. Our home was located at the top of the village and enjoyed the longest light. We were one of five black landowner families in Cenyu, and like everyone who owned land back then, we grew mealies and had a piggery and a kraal for cows on our relatively large plot (close to 4 000 square metres). Belonging to my paternal grandmother, Mangangenkomo, our plot also was home to Cenyu's only general dealer shop, Ngqika Store, which my grandmother had named after a great eighteenth century Xhosa king, Ngqika ka Mlawu.

My mother, Yolisa NoDumo Njoli (née Ntuthu), was a lively, social and smartly dressed operator. She was a woman whose presence you sensed immediately when she walked into a room, not least because she always wore a beautiful floral perfume. She also was incredibly hard working and a real disciplinarian. A teacher by training, she was a businesswoman by inclination, running three successful businesses – the general dealer, a tuck shop, and a shebeen – while also teaching fulltime at Nomathemba Primary School.

Born in 1942, my mother, like me, had grown up on a farm outside Stutterheim. Her mother, Rhoda Mamvulane Ntuthu, née Ntshoko (also a teacher), was my grandfather's fourth wife (after three previous marriages didn't last), making my mother the youngest of about ten siblings. When she married my father, Victor Mthunzi Njoli, in 1963 at the age of 20, my mother came under the wing of my paternal grandmother, Elizabeth Vuyelwa Njoli. As it is in most cultures, your mother-in-law becomes your new mother with far-reaching influence into your marriage and acceptability within the new family. These relationships can either strengthen or break your marriage.

In our community people gave names to chiefs and male leaders, but my paternal grandmother, Vuyelwa, whom I called makhulu, was known as

Mangangenkomo or 'the one who is as strong as an ox' by everyone else. Large both in stature and accomplishment, my grandmother was a giant in my eyes. A respected businesswoman known all the way to East London (where she was a business trader and property owner in the township of kuTsolo), she was an entrepreneur way ahead of her time. Although I was only six when she died in 1970, I remember her as very strict but also extremely good with people: respect for others and proper greetings were non-negotiables. She was also very outspoken and always communicated in a straightforward manner.

Widowed in her early 40s, my grandmother called the shots in her life as if she were a man. She ran her businesses; drank, sat, and talked with men; and even built her own church within our homestead, a large beautiful rondavel. Looking back, I suspect that the latter move was to avoid being talked about in the pulpits as much as to control the preaching (she held weekly planning meetings with the preacher and I remember once hearing her comment that she did not like long sermons). Nurturing the enterprising spirit already instilled by my mother's own mother uMaMvulane (who in addition to being a teacher was involved with the Presbyterian Women's Guild and YWCA), my paternal grandmother mentored my mother, whom she loved almost as fiercely as my father did.

My father, Victor Mthunzi Njoli, was a journalist and he worked for *Imvo Zabantsundu* newspaper in King William's Town. His life was all too brief, however, and it ended when he was only 32. The man I remember was gentle, fun-loving, and deeply devoted to my mother. He was also a keen sportsman (I found tennis racquets and books about karate among his things years after his death) and a lover of choral music. Constantly listening to the radio, particularly the classical stations, he instilled his love of music in me, and some of my fondest memories are of accompanying him to the choral music competitions that came to our area.

He was also a lay deacon in the Anglican church. He had wanted to enter the seminary and to that end had gone back to school, earning his matric in the same year he fell ill with cancer of the liver. With my father's sudden death in 1972, my mother, aged 28, with children aged three months to eight years old, realised she would have to be mother and father to us three. Fortunately, my grandmother had left my mother both the Ngqika Store and a bold example to follow.

Ngqika Store

Due to its richness, the strip of farmland between Kings William's Town and Cathcart, of which Stutterheim was a part, was excluded from the old Transkei and Ciskei homelands. In its efforts to remove black people from such 'white corridors', the apartheid government had made it impossible for black people to participate in the land market processes of the times. As such, my grandmother could never transfer the title deed to my family's land and the general dealer shop where I grew up to my parents, and it remains in her name to this day.

I started working in our store at the age of eight, effectively becoming my mother's right-hand 'woman' when my father died. After school I would come home to relieve Sis Nobandla, who worked the till, taking my place in my chair that was a big box stacked with cushions so I could reach the counter. There I sat, working the cash register until my mother came home from teaching around 4pm. Together we would repack shelves, take stock and work on accounts in the late afternoon lull before the last rush of shoppers charged through on their way home from work to buy things such as bread, candles and paraffin before we closed at 7pm.

Every morning before getting ready for school, I would open the shop at 6am to receive the fresh warm bread, delivered to us from the bakery in town. In the days before she bought her car, my mother would catch a lift with the bakery van to take her back into town, where she bought fresh vegetables from the market to stock the shop before starting her teaching day. We sold everything from single boxes of matches to 20 kilogramme sacks of mealie meal, all of which we measured out from behind the counter. After school I'd cut pieces of the long blue soap that was popular in those days, always making sure to get six squares from a single block. Pumping paraffin into bottles and cutting the tight long rolls of chew tobacco into half-cent size pieces that filled an airtight container were my most hated chores, as they left a stink that lingered on my hands no matter how much I washed them.

Although I never played sports or had time to be idle, the shop, which was located in our yard, was a kind of playground for me. Kids from the village often came over, both to play and to 'help', and my mother always treated 'assistants' to fruit and snacks. In the moments when the shop was quiet I would curl up in a corner to read. Having found a box of my father's old comics, I relished those peaceful afternoons with Archie and Andy Capp, the latter having been my dad's favourite. This dearly loved pastime was also the only activity my mother would not disturb, except to indulge her favourite moment of the day, which was when I would read aloud to her from the daily newspaper. As a teacher she insisted on the importance of keeping up with the news and knowing what was happening in the rest of the world.

⬦⬦⬦⬦⬦

Although I enjoyed seeing people coming and going and hearing the village gossip at the shop, I occasionally resented the fact that other kids got to play while I had to work all the time.

'They are able to play because their parents are working somewhere where somebody else is paying them. In your situation, if you're not working here, who is going to pay your school fees? Who is going to pay me?' my mother would say, reminding me that I didn't have a father, and so this was what we had to do.

I came to accept that this was how our family operated and that complaining would get me nowhere. Mostly I wasn't bothered, but I do remember one winter when my Aunt Zet, whom I was very close to, came to visit. Lamenting the fact that I had to open the shop so early in the cold mornings while other children were still sleeping, I think the thing that really got to her was my insistence that if my father was alive this would not be happening.

Naturally Aunt Zet spoke to my mother, but her suggestion that my mom use a lighter touch with me completely backfired. When I got home from school that day, my mother ordered me into the car and drove us straight to the graveyard.

'This is where your father is, so stop complaining about your father as if you don't know where yours is. Other children don't have fathers, they don't even know where they are. Yours, at least you know where he is,' she said, before invoking Winnie Mandela.

My mother had deep respect for Mama Winnie, often reminding my siblings and me that although her husband had died, she could at least point to his grave, while Winnie endured a far worse fate with her husband 'buried alive' on Robben Island.

'I must never ever hear you complain about your life again,' she concluded.

Although that episode might strike some as harsh, my mother's staunch refusal to feel sorry for herself and the awareness that things can always be worse became the foundation of my later view – both in my career and personal life – that the glass is always half full.

My mother was also a great motivator. Because we worked for ourselves, she regularly set clear goals and guidelines to strive towards. For instance, she would tell us that she wanted to buy a car in six months' time, so we all then worked together towards that target. Or she would say, 'I'm saving for school fees because I want to send you to that private school, Bethel College.' She drew a clear line between what we were working for and the outcome or benefit of that work. As a result, I have always been conscious of the direct link between the effort and quality of what you put into something and the output that results. To this day, I am grateful for the work ethic my mother drilled into me from such an early age, and I suspect it was key in shaping my ability to buckle down and get on with a task when required.

Special treatment

I was fortunate to have enjoyed a very happy and privileged childhood – I felt so then and still feel this way now. Our house was a hive of activity, located on the main road by the taxi and bus stop. When my grandmother was still alive and for quite some years after she passed, the villagers would come to our church on Sundays, after which we served huge cooked lunches. Between the people working in the shop and elsewhere on our property (on the farm, chopping wood, cleaning the house, etc.), the frequent drop-in visitors, and constant semi-permanent visitors like my cousins (of whom there were always at least a few staying for anywhere from two weeks to two years), our home buzzed with a positive and dynamic energy. Ours was a home in which there were always biscuits or a cake in the oven because you never knew when visitors might appear, and when guests arrived we knew to just make tea, not waiting for anyone to ask.

Much as I enjoyed the constant activity that defined our home, I was by nature a shy and self-conscious child. People I didn't know constantly recognised me as 'that child from the shop', which made me even more self-conscious. Luckily our home was large, with quite a few outside rooms. When even that space became too busy, I escaped by saying that I was going to clean my grandmother's church. While dusting the chairs, I would take a break to read the Presbyterian hymn books. As much as the church was a refuge to find some quiet, I also sought that private contemplative feeling you sometimes encounter in holy spaces. When my father was still alive we used to go to the Anglican church where he was a deacon. Arriving early, he would tell me I could play with the other kids outside, but I generally preferred to sit inside the church, enjoying the peace before the congregants arrived. I associated spirituality with peace, tranquillity and contemplation.

◇◇◇◇◇

For all of my responsibilities at the shop, I also knew I was treated specially. This 'special treatment' took different forms, starting with the fact that my mother dressed me in fancy clothes and I was one of the few children at school with shoes (more often than not I'd remove them as soon as I got there).

While it was the norm for children in those days to walk to school on their own, my mother sent someone with me for the two-kilometre walk there, and at the end of the day someone came to fetch me. My mother likes to tell a story about a rainy day when she decided to pick me up from school herself. I had already begun walking back home with a group of kids – nine-year-olds, giggling and singing – when she drove past in her bakkie. Hiding from the heavy downpour under blankets and towels, we didn't notice it was her. When her bakkie passed again, someone said, 'It's Dumo's car.'

My mother stopped and shouted for us to get in the back. We quickly piled in, still under our blankets. She only realised I was among the children in the back when we got home. Needless to say, she was upset that I hadn't waited to be fetched, and then hadn't said anything when I got into the bakkie. As much as I was aware of my family's relative privilege in our community, like any child, I just wanted to fit in.

There were other more complex ways that I felt the privilege, power and choices that came with my mother's status as an independent and financially secure businesswoman. Businesspeople in the town – meaning white people, as well as black business and community leaders in our village and elsewhere – all knew my mother, who was out in the world doing things normally done by men, just like Mangangenkomo had taught her.

The success of the businesses she ran meant that we lived a stable middle-class life. Our house had an inside bathroom and electricity, which my mother had installed using a diesel generator for the power. My siblings and I all went to semi-private schools, and our family took Christmas holidays away by the sea in Hamburg, close to the town of Peddie, where my Aunt Lungisa was the town manager. My mother also purchased her own car. In those days as a black woman, you could not enter into a contract without a man vouching for you, and so even though she had the money, when she bought her first car (a white Toyota bakkie), she had to get her brother who worked in East London to vouch for her. When she bought her second car a year later – a VW Passat sedan – the dealership waived this absurd system, by then aware that she was the car's real owner, which was a big deal at that time.

My mother's financial security not only provided for my relatively comfortable upbringing, but also demonstrated the way economic power gives you choices and affects how people treat you. This was made very clear every time we went to do errands in Stutterheim town. Although I was aware of the race issues of the day and knew that there were certain things black people were allowed or not allowed to do in town, my mother's position as a businesswoman sheltered me from many of the daily indignities of apartheid. Despite the existence of separate queues for black and white, when we went to places like the bank, the bank manager would open a special queue for us because of the size of my mother's transactions (we always came with a lot of two and five cent coins). It was the same at the butchery and post office, where they knew that 'the people from Ngqika Store' were very busy and were good customers.

When I needed clothes in preparation for boarding school, I remember Elizabeth's Fashions was the only clothing boutique in our small town. Because black customers couldn't go inside if they were not buying, the owner would give our driver a box of clothes for my mother and me to try on appro (customer approval). Fitting them and keeping what we wanted, we would send the rest back, allowing her white customers to remain ignorant of the fact that those garments had touched black skin.

In these ways, I was sheltered from some of the harsh realities that other black people faced. Even so, we did not escape the 'in your face' discrimination of things such as the 'Blacks Only' signs prominently displayed on all doors, from the corner café (called tea rooms at the time) to the bus station and even the doctor's rooms. In most places, no matter how much money you had, as a black person you had to stand in the queue meant for you and wait while white customers were served first.

In addition to the overt discrimination I saw outside our home, interactions in the shop also made me acutely aware of how little most black people had. First were the people constantly coming to the shop wanting to buy food for which they didn't have enough money, resulting in a lot of our sales happening on credit. Also, because the shop had the only telephone in the village, people frequently came to us to call their relatives. With the majority of black households in Cenyu leasing their lands, almost every family had someone working away as labour in the cities or mines, and so I was also often asked to write letters for people who were illiterate. A typical letter would go like this: 'Dear So and So, ikati ilele eziko' (even the cat is now sleeping on top of the stove [since there is no food]) ... Finally, because of our access to the phone, we would sometimes be woken at night in emergencies, and asked to call either the police or an ambulance for someone critically ill. A few times I remember my mother having to drive the person to hospital herself because the telephone operator would just ignore the calls from our number. Through all of this, I became familiar with people's struggles and circumstances – deaths in the family and no money for the burial, families depending on monthly remittances from a son or brother or husband who suddenly stopped sending them – and as a result I developed an acute and early awareness of the poverty and inequality in our community.

My consciousness of this suffering and wish to do something about it were behind my desire to become a social worker, a job I first heard about from sis Phumla Maqubela, a distant relative I met at a family wedding. I thought of Phumla as very sophisticated and interesting, and when she spoke about her job helping to change people's lives at Child Welfare, I was intrigued. All of this appealed to me greatly, and I decided that I too would become a social worker.

For all my desire to 'help', I had no real clue as to what was going on in South Africa at the time. In those days, Nelson Mandela's face remained a mystery, the mention of banned people or singing of *Nkosi Sikelel' iAfrika* was forbidden, and politics was only discussed in whispers, if at all. One of the few instances I can recall hearing anything vaguely 'political' was the morning of the 1976 Soweto school riots. I was in Standard 5 (now Grade 7), and my mother, who had been listening to the radio, woke me even earlier than usual.

'Why are you still sleeping? They are killing our children in Soweto!' she said, bursting into my room, uncharacteristically flustered.

When she took me to school that morning, the teachers weren't sure if class was being held, but as there was no TV, we didn't really know what was going on. In the weeks that followed our teachers asked us if we were happy to learn in Afrikaans, and when it was time to write our exam papers, we were given the choice of writing in English. Although we knew the riots were triggered by the issue of Afrikaans instruction in the classroom, politics remained a no-go zone except to the extent that my mother spoke of Winnie Mandela's bravery as a 'widow'.

It was only much later that I realised that my mother quietly had been doing her part for years. Because our house was constantly filled with different people, we never thought much of who was around – you didn't know whether this person was here to sell chickens, pick up a pig, or attend a teachers' meeting. I certainly never imagined my mother was assisting the political underground in her own small ways, and had no clue when I went away to boarding school the following year that she dealt with her fair share of police harassment, especially during the consumer boycott campaign that spread around Stutterheim and the Eastern Cape in the late 1970s. It was not an era to go around advertising that you were a comrade.

CHAPTER 2

Bethel College

Boarding school was the norm in my family, so I was thrilled when at the age of twelve my turn came to leave home and attend Bethel College, a Seventh-Day Adventist boarding school outside Butterworth (eGcuwa), in the then Transkei homeland. Run independently of the apartheid government, mission or church schools were where black people went for a good holistic education in those days. Although Bethel College only accepted Seventh-Day Adventist children, my indomitable mother had found a way to get me a place. Calling on our old family friend Dr Babini Maliza, whose father's farm shared a property boundary with the school, my mother managed not only to get an application form, but also to convince the school that accepting me would be the neighbourly thing to do.

The Bethel College campus was beautiful, nestled in a lush isolated valley and boasting impressive buildings from boarding houses to a dining hall to a graceful chapel. As the only high school for black Seventh-Day Adventists in southern Africa, Bethel's student body was pan-African, its 300 or so students coming from Malawi, Zimbabwe and Lesotho, as well as all the South African provinces. Meeting so many children from other parts of Africa made a big impression on me at the time, and also ensured that I learned to speak proper Sesotho, Tswana and Zulu. Bethel's internationalism was further enhanced by the fact that 70% of our teachers were white missionaries, hailing mostly from North America and Europe. All in all, Bethel College was a nurturing and peaceful space that embraced diversity and lived by its motto: 'We grow you spiritually, mentally and physically'.

I was at Bethel for Forms 1 to 5, which were ages twelve to seventeen. In my family of teachers, education was a given, as was the expectation that I would be the first in my family to attend university and earn a higher degree. Although the primary school where I had been in the top of my class was a simple village school, complete with mud rondavels and thatched roofs, I grew up in a house filled with books and magazines, with a mother who was a teacher and businessperson, and so Bethel's rigorous academic standards did not come as a shock. In fact, my classmates at Bethel came from middle-class backgrounds similar to my own, and I loved no longer sticking out as a 'special' child.

In addition to its strong academics (including numerous electives from macramé to stargazing to motor mechanics), the school instilled the value of physical work. Manual labour was compulsory and strictly observed on non-Sabbath days. As Form 1 students we were part of the campus cleaning crew and did everything from cleaning the schoolyard to working the fields and woodwork.

From a spiritual perspective, in addition to attending church all the time (and all day on Saturdays, when Adventists observe the Sabbath), Bethel focused on simple and virtuous living. During the school term we lived in a bubble where neither radio nor TV were allowed, except for once a quarter when we were shown a movie that was either a musical or a National Geographic documentary. Our one creative indulgence, then, was the spiritual outlet of choral music.

I had always loved choral music, and that passion was encouraged both by the environment of the college and the attentions of my first mentor. Miss Victoria Smondile was the matron for the girls' hostel. Smart, independent, and single, this well-dressed disciplinarian in her late 30s reminded me of my mother. In fact, when my mother first brought me to the school, Miss Smondile – who knew that we were not Seventh-Day Adventists and wanted to be sure I would fit in – made a point of chatting to my mother. They got along well, and Smondile always kept an eye out for me.

In addition to serving as hostel matron, Smondile was my Xhosa teacher in junior high school (Forms 1 to 3). She spoke beautiful Xhosa and cultivated my appreciation for the rich expressiveness of our shared mother tongue. Among our student body at Bethel there were not many native Xhosa speakers who really understood what lies behind Xhosa idioms, and I loved discussing the original meanings of those sayings with Smondile. E.W.M. Mesatywa's book *Izaci namaqhalo esiXhosa* (Xhosa idioms and sayings) was our favourite book in this regard. Smondile also encouraged my passion for music. Amongst the Seventh-Day Adventist choirs, Bethel's was known to be one of the best, performing all the classics from Handel's *Messiah* to Michael Haydn's Hymns. Twice a year, our choirmaster Mr Yaze held auditions in the chapel, and for three years I showed up to audition every six months. But for all my passion, I lacked musical talent, a fact that Mr Yaze clearly noted in his efforts to chase me away. After a few years of this there was actually a joke among the teachers about 'that one who likes to audition for choir but can't sing'.

As a Form 4 student, cleaning the chapel had become part of my chores. I loved this job, not only because it was one of the easiest, but also because it meant spending the whole afternoon listening to the choir practising to the organist's accompaniment. I would lose myself in the music while also learning the songs.

When the second auditions came that year, I put my name on the list as usual.

'No, no, no. Don't put your name on that list,' Mr Yaze said when he saw me.

'But I know all the songs,' I insisted.

Despite his reluctance, Mr Yaze let me audition. Then to everyone's great surprise, I made it in. I'm pretty sure Smondile intervened, asking Mr Yaze to just give me *anything* to do. My participation came with conditions, however, including standing at a particular angle in the 60-person choir, and not singing too loudly. I happily agreed to everything, which is how, to the horror of my friends who knew I couldn't sing, I became part of the choir.

This experience demonstrated how tenacity, determination and simply getting in the room can make the impossible, possible. I think it also speaks to some quality that over the years that has caused me to be in spaces where people wondered to themselves, How did she get there? I have always had this attitude that if I really feel like I should be somewhere, I will find a way.

Good works

Over the five years I spent at Bethel College, my exposure to great teachers caused my interest in being a social worker to transform into a desire to teach. My favourite subjects were English, Xhosa and Business Economics. I particularly loved the practicality of Business Economics and how it gave name, shape and sense to what I had been doing all those years at our general dealer store. It was affirming to realise how much I already knew about topics like marketing and the differences between retail and wholesale pricing.

Bethel College was also where I started to gain confidence in speaking my mind. I went from being a child who was terrified of being called on or speaking in front of others to leading classes at Sabbath School, where I also learned I could have my views challenged without feeling sensitive. Having come from a village school where you rarely heard contrasting positions on a topic, I now encountered people who readily challenged my opinions, and I found I loved those robust discussions and the open environment that fostered them.

Another big development for me in those years was the decision to convert to Seventh-Day Adventism. By the time I was in Form 3, I had come to find great meaning in the Adventist approach to religion and spirituality. One of the biggest points in Adventism was that God created humans with the ability to choose our actions. The message was that if you find yourself in Hell, it was not because you were born with sin, but rather because you made poor choices. This appealed to my long-held belief that we are not innocent bystanders in our own lives, but rather that we each have a role to play in changing or shaping our individual journeys.

Adventism provided very practical clear guidelines about what it meant to be a Christian and how to prepare for the afterlife. As an Adventist you had a responsibility to live a self-examined life, always asking if you were worthy of being called a child of God. Worthiness meant living a life beyond reproach, which required, on the one hand, giving certain things up, and on the other, engaging in good works. We spent our Saturday afternoons visiting the sick or elderly and performing chores like helping to clean people's houses and fetch water. Imbued with something of a missionary spirit, you did good works in part so that people could see the goodness of God through those works, which in turn might inspire them to convert.

All of this resonated with my own deeply held sense of responsibility both to take control of one's own life and to help others. I never related to the philosophy that 'stuff' just happens *to* you. Instead I always believed in cultivating a sense of control, even if it was as small as the choice of waking up and washing your face. I knew there were situations and circumstances beyond people's control, but as Mandela later showed us, you could choose how you responded to those situations. Even in prison, he and his comrades decided how to engage with the guards, and therefore chose lives of dignity. Adventist doctrine supported this perspective and gave me a foundation from which I could look at any situation no matter how bad and ask myself what I could do to make myself or the situation feel or even just appear better.

Finally, Adventism also assisted me with a dilemma I had faced since childhood. All my life I had been aware (sometimes embarrassingly) of the privilege of having in abundance that which others did not have at all. It started when I was the only child in my class wearing shoes or a nice jersey, and continued at the shop, where I faced hungry people without money to buy food. I hated that I was supposed to tell a person with no money to come back only when she had something in her pocket, while we had bread on our shelves.

Instead I would often tell people to return at the end of the day when, if there was something left over, I could give it to them instead of swapping it with the bakery for fresh loaves the next day. Or I would suggest that the person help clean the shop or do something so I could 'give' them bread and milk. I always tried to find a way to share what we had, even though inevitably my actions got back to my mother, who would look at me with exasperation, asking why I was giving away her profit. In Adventism, I found a framework affirming that helping was a God-given responsibility.

I was sixteen when I decided to convert. Conversion required signing up to take a set of classes to prepare for my baptism – something for which I needed parental permission. When I brought it up on my weekly phone call with my mother she refused as she saw my move from being an Anglican to Seventh-Day Adventism as leaving my father's church behind. For weeks she continued to say no, which of course only strengthened my resolve. A few weeks before I came home for the December holidays, I wrote a long letter explaining my reasons for conversion, and when I came home, she saw just how adamant I was: I had become a vegetarian, wasn't interested in listening to non-religious music, and had become very much a born-again type Christian. Her response to all this was to invite Reverend Mcilongo, a very close family friend and the Anglican priest who had confirmed me when I was ten, to come and speak to me.

Tata Mcilongo and I had always got on well. After my father had passed away, he and his wife, aunt Mpumi, had been like a second family. Over the course of a few weeks, he came over and we had long talks in which he tried to understand why I wanted to convert. One of our big debates was around the fact that I wasn't going to church on Sunday, but rather observing Sabbath on Saturday. My insistence on the Saturday Sabbath was an issue with my mother, who was always very busy in the shop that day and wanted my help. By our third conversation, Tata Mcilongo and I were basically having a Bible study.

'I've learned so much from you about the Bible and have enjoyed hearing how you see and interpret it. I can see this is not just a fad, and I actually think it doesn't matter which religion you choose, as you are clearly serious in your Bible study,' he said before recommending that my mother allow me to convert. To her great credit, not only did my mother allow my conversion, she would bring me Adventist books and religious music to enjoy on my Saturday Sabbaths.

Although in a few years I would no longer identify as an Adventist (these days I find my spirituality in many places, including recognition of my ancestors), this experience proved the value of doing your homework when trying to bring someone around to your point of view, as well as the importance of sticking to your convictions and values.

A cruel system

With my schoolmates hailing from townships like Soweto, Langa and Gugulethu, I started to hear stories about what was happening out in the world. It was at Bethel College that I first came to understand the deeper reasons behind the 1976 school riots, and with that the first seeds of political awareness were planted in me.

My personal understanding of the riots had been limited to the objection around Afrikaans as the language of instruction in black schools. Now I learned that this had been a signpost gesturing to the larger injustice of the intentional inferiority of black children's education. I learned that the legislation behind so-called Bantu education specified the need for black children to have a poor education in order to preclude the possibility that we might expect or be capable of being more than 'hewers of wood and drawers of water', as apartheid's chief architect H.F. Verwoerd put it.

For the first time I understood how the education system was structured to exclude us as economic players, except to the extent that we could do menial tasks for white people. I had seen the economic results of this non-education on the lives of people in Cenyu – both those living there and the ones whose stories I knew from reading their letters. Grasping the extent to which poor education perpetuated the cycle of poverty and lack of choice, and how the riots had been about challenging the whole political system that wilfully kept black people in ignorance was a turning point for me.

It was with this knowledge that I came home for the December holidays in 1980. I was helping my mother with some shop admin when I found in the drawer where she kept receipts, a thick stack of gift vouchers with different rand face values. I took them to my mother and asked her what they were.

'Those are such a problem,' she said, making a face.

She went on to explain that the vouchers belonged to a well-connected businessman by the name of Jack. One of the town's bigger employers, this Jack owned a brick-making factory employing about a hundred people, as well as some general dealer shops. He also had interests in a few liquor stores. Jack paid his employees exclusively in vouchers, which could only be used in places where he had arrangements and deals. From the butcher to the doctor, a number of white businesses accepted the vouchers. Not having any such deal, my mother as a rule did not accept Jack's vouchers as payment, but sometimes a desperate customer would come with only these vouchers, promising to exchange them for real money later. This was how over time my mother ended up with a stack of Jack's vouchers. Eventually she went to Jack to ask for her money. With great reluctance he agreed to give her some cash but told her not to return. The cycle continued though, and my mother once again found herself with this useless currency.

After we had this conversation, my mother called Jack and told him that I was home from boarding school and she needed money to buy things for me as well as stock for her store. Jack agreed to let her use the vouchers to buy the stock she needed from one of his shops, but at retail, not wholesale prices. Understanding that this was the most she was going to get out of him, my mother accepted.

'Why don't you take this to the police?' I asked, shocked at her acceptance.

'And what do you think the police will do?' she said, giving me a long and resigned look.

I wanted her to question and challenge what this man was doing, but she stopped me. 'Don't ask so many questions. I still have to live with these people and run my business,' she said, ending the conversation.

At the time she was running an unlicensed shebeen and tuck shop, about which Jack and his cronies no doubt knew. Suddenly I saw that as a single widow and a black woman, my mother could be bullied by the likes of Jack, who with a word could see that her general dealer licence, for which she had to reapply yearly, was rejected.

It was in this moment that I started to comprehend how insidious, innovative and cruel the apartheid system was. How it was constructed to work only for white people like Jack to control black people, including the likes of my mother. This was the turning point for me and later when confronted by the stats on lower black stock exchange ownership in our country, I would often wonder how much ownership Jack's family and associates had on the exchange, and whether they appreciated or at least understood how their world was built.

CHAPTER 3

Finding my freedom

University had always been part of my mother's plan for me. She instilled in me from an early age not only how important an education is but also the need to be self-sufficient and independent. And she was clear about the order of things: get an education first and then a good husband.

So in 1982 at the age of eighteen I arrived at the University of Fort Hare in Alice. Fort Hare was the obvious choice. As a black student you either went to Fort Hare in the Eastern Cape, Ohlange in KwaZulu-Natal, or the University of the North in Limpopo. Although I had considered applying for a scholarship to a Seventh-Day Adventist university in the USA, my mother's continued reservations about my conversion kept me closer to home.

This was probably for the best, as my Adventism fell away in that first year of new experiences. Free from the confines of a strict regimen of work and prohibitions – first those dictated by my mother, and then the ones I had adopted at Bethel College – it was an exhilarating and social time. Thanks to my exposure to Sotho, Zulu and Tswana, it was easy for me to make new friends, and I revelled in the student life. Engaging in activities like ballroom dancing and beauty contests (the latter mostly to annoy my mother, whom I knew would disapprove), I started wearing jewellery and dresses that came above the knee, then going to parties, and eventually even drinking alcohol, none of which were allowed for a good Adventist. The thrill of all these new interactions with people from different places filled me with an elating sense of the breadth of the world and its possibilities.

From an academic standpoint, I was not the best student to begin with. I still remember how amazing it felt to wake up knowing I could skip class if I chose. Experiencing such freedom for the first time, though negative academically, was empowering psychologically. I spent those first years finding myself through rebelling and socialising, all against the backdrop of Fort Hare, which at that time was a hotbed of political activism.

While I was never actively involved in politics at Fort Hare, you could not be at the university and remain unaware of what was going on in the country at large. Those were the years of the homeland governments' most ruthless political suppression and, as the hub of student resistance, Fort Hare was a target. Former Special Branch agent General Charles Sebe, who was Ciskei head of Intelligence and worked directly with the government in Pretoria, was a perpetually menacing presence. Stories about student interrogations circulated constantly, and we experienced boycotts and strikes to which the police often responded with brutality, whether on or off campus. Liberated from my sheltered upbringing, I started to understand how profound poverty and brutal authoritarianism were not unique to any single community, but were manifestations of the larger apartheid system and experienced by black people everywhere, often to a much worse degree than anything I had ever glimpsed.

My newly found freedom and carefree behaviour in my first year as a student resulted in what I might describe as my first public failure – and with this came lessons I never forgot. Unsurprisingly, I did not perform well academically in my first year. In fact, that is an understatement. When my results arrived at home by post, my mother and I opened them with great expectations, which quickly turned to disbelief. I was confronted with the cold reality that I had only passed one subject out of the five that I wrote that year. Although poor results were not unexpected, I was bitterly disappointed all the same. I sobbed for the whole afternoon, until my mother called off the pity party.

'Kubhubhe bani?'(Who has died?) she demanded. Then, without waiting for me to respond, she continued: 'So between you and me, who should be wailing the loudest? I've lost money paying your university tuition, yet you are the chief crier. What exactly have you lost?"

This sharp and accurate reprimand brought me back to my senses. As usual, my mother was right.

The hard-hitting truth was that I was mortified and embarrassed. Everyone in our large household, which included my mother's customers in the village, had been waiting to hear my results. It was also a sober reminder that my success was a burden that I carried for the whole village and not just an individual achievement. This was later borne out in my professional ascendancy. How I could let myself down like this was beyond me. My first public failure was a bitter pill to swallow.

Getting serious

Academically it took me a while to find my footing. With my plans to become a teacher, I entered Fort Hare as a Bachelor of Pedagogics student in the commerce stream. Despite having a good head for the ideas behind business economics, the numbers themselves did not speak to me, and I failed accounting three times in my first two years. Worried that I would never graduate, I returned to my original interest in social work, switching to a BA in psychology at the end of my second year.

My second year was also when I met Presto Fakude, my future husband. Originally from Kwa-Thema in Springs, Presto was a handsome and smart post-grad doing an Honours degree in chemistry. At 27, he was eight years my senior and had worked in the real world, and his maturity appealed to me. We dated for nearly three years before marrying in 1986, after he finished his Master of Science degree in chemistry.

My mother was extremely bothered by my marriage to an 'older man' who already had two degrees and was 'from Joburg' to boot – the negative connotations of the big city speaking for themselves in her mind. She still saw me as a child and she felt she had not fully prepared me for this stage of life. She agreed to my marriage on the condition that we not start a family until I had completed my first degree, which she was still funding.

'As a woman you need to have a degree certificate before considering a marriage certificate,' she insisted – rightly, as I would agree.

My mother's concern for my independence as a woman was well founded, although at the time I probably did not realise just how valid it was. That said, I was not completely ignorant. Having taken a temporary job in the child maintenance office at the magistrate's office in Zwelitsha, King William's Town during my second-year December holidays, I spent a month watching women coming to collect court-ordered maintenance payments from the fathers of their children.

Every morning I would arrive to a long queue of mothers. One by one, they supplied their details to me. Going through the daily list, all too often I found myself saying things like, 'Sorry, your husband didn't pay,' or 'Your husband is no longer working there.' The women's faces would crumple with defeat and anxiety. Often they asked where the man in question had gone, but of course I didn't know. Or they confided, 'This is the second month he hasn't paid. I don't know what to do.' Their desperation was palpable. I would try to console them and answer their questions, but there was nothing I could really do. At some point my supervisor admonished me, saying I was taking too long with the ladies, and that I should just tell them the money was not there and move on.

I remember an incident when a particular lady came twice in one week. Recognising her from a few days before, I asked if there had been a problem with her payment.

'No, I've got two kids. This is for my other child from a different father,' she explained.

Because each company's maintenance payments (often garnished from wages) were paid out on a particular day of the week – government on Mondays, private companies on Tuesdays – this sort of thing was entirely plausible. But in that moment, I was struck by the indignity of the situation and felt two things very strongly. One, a fierce conviction that I must never allow myself to be put in such a position. And two, anger at all the men who did not pay maintenance for their own children.

The frequency of non-payment struck me as a form of abuse: that you could separate from someone but that person could still exert control over you through this maintenance grant was horrific to me. The whole experience highlighted the necessity of financial independence, not only for practical reasons, but also to maintain one's dignity in the world.

The other thing I learned at this job was that when you are on the other side of the counter from someone who is vulnerable – because they are in financial or emotional distress – what a simple but important act of kindness it is to pay the person the respect of being heard or listened to. I didn't care how long the queue was, I could never just say, 'Next, move along,' to a person who was already down.

◇◇◇◇◇

Notwithstanding the fact that I was only one year from completing my junior degree, I had been at Fort Hare for five years and university policy dictated I move on. There were a lot of strikes at the time, and I think the administration was conscious of preventing students from lingering too long. Thus in 1987 I transferred to the University of Transkei (UNITRA) in Umtata.

Originally a branch of Fort Hare, which was still run by a white administration, UNITRA had been an independent institution since 1977. It was a vibrant intellectual hub where black people were visibly in charge, with over 70% of UNITRA's academic staff hailing from the rest of the continent. The vice-chancellor, Professor Wiseman Nkuhlu, who was the first African in South Africa to become a chartered accountant, ran the university with a clear pan-African vision of developing black intellectuals who could hold their own anywhere in the world.

Despite its location in the homelands, Umtata was an artsy yet cosmopolitan university town, where I found its vibrant social and political environment a breath of fresh air. Buzzing with black professionals and business people, it was a destination for Joburg and Soweto socialites when they wanted to go somewhere happening for a weekend, and it was a place where it felt like black people were visibly running their own lives.

It was at UNITRA in 1988 that I completed my Bachelor of Arts degree in psychology, English and education and also truly fell in love with learning. Unlike Fort Hare, where an underlying tension infused a campus whose white administrators were not inclined to encourage students' freedom either academically or culturally, the atmosphere at UNITRA was one of openness. You could feel that lecturers not only encouraged discussion, but even required that we held and articulated different views.

Because we had promised my mother that I would complete my degree before we had children, it became clear that after I was academically excluded from Fort Hare that I had to complete my degree elsewhere. As a result, during my two years at UNITRA I commuted back and forth between Umtata and Alice, where Presto had taken a lecturing post in chemistry at Fort Hare. Going home on month ends, we spent our time within a circle of friends for whom frequent and lively philosophical discussions were the norm. Between debating the topics of the day at UNITRA, and engaging with our group of friends in Alice, I began to notice that I held firmer views than others, and that people listened to my perspective. My confidence – which had first emerged at Bethel College – grew to the point where I realised I actually enjoyed expressing myself and being listened to, and for the first time started to see myself as a possible leader.

Meanwhile my resolve around having a career also strengthened. I knew many women who had earned a degree before marrying, but then dropped out of the professional world. I felt increasingly sure that that would not be my path: I wanted to be out in the world, stimulated and challenged by a career, even if I did not yet know the shape it would take.

In search of life experience

Having finished my BA at UNITRA, I returned to Fort Hare in 1989 to complete an Honours degree in psychology. It was my fourth year of marriage to Presto, and having made good on my promise to my mother to first complete my junior degree, we decided to start a family. I fell pregnant quickly but I managed to finish my Honours degree and apply to do a Master's in clinical psychology at Rhodes University before my due date.

My desire to become a clinical psychologist was largely inspired by one of my most dynamic lecturers at UNITRA, the amazingly bright and incisive thinker Dr Pumla Gobodo. Later she would serve as a commissioner on the Truth and Reconciliation Commission (TRC) and author numerous books (including *A Human Being Died That Night*, about her interviews with infamous apartheid assassin Eugene de Kock). Gobodo's approach wove African culture into traditional psychology, and focused on practical applications to the issues that our communities and society faced at the time. She made the field appear a dazzling and fulfilling challenge, and I was thrilled by the idea of joining the likes of her ranks.

In October 1989, my son Phila was born. Unfortunately, my joy at becoming a mother was tempered not long after my child's birth by the hugely disappointing news that I had not been accepted to the Master's programme at Rhodes. The department cited a lack of 'life experience' as the reason, explaining that those accepted already had work experience and the average age in the class was 30. While some people suggested that I just enjoy my 'time off' with my baby, I knew that wouldn't work for me. Surrounded by people with advanced degrees and having begun to embrace my professional ambitions, I suddenly found myself with nothing to do but care for a small baby. I felt stuck.

Meanwhile, change was apace all around me. It was the end of 1989, and even though we did not know it at the time, parliament was about to unban all political parties and release Nelson Mandela from prison. That said, people still were regularly arrested, banished from campus, or simply disappeared, and political discussions remained shrouded in secrecy. While always supportive of my academic and career interests, Presto had taken it upon himself to shelter me from politics. He would go out but wouldn't tell me where and wouldn't 'let' me come. 'There are no women there,' or 'It's too dangerous,' he would say.

Coming from my mother's house, where there was nothing I could not do as a woman, this behaviour left me feeling excluded and patronised. I had never personally viewed my gender as a barrier to anything, and I would get outraged when I sometimes heard men speaking about women as if we were weak or incapable. I had been raised by women who made their own money and were active participants in their own lives. I could not relate to any other paradigm. On the contrary, in the home where I was raised, if there was a cow or pig to be slaughtered, I was in the scrum with the guys, helping to select the animal.

The day before my graduation in Umtata, we had bought a sheep to slaughter for a braai. While Presto and the other men were having a good time drinking, the sheep remained very much alive. I was getting annoyed because we needed to clean the meat and start cooking, and I didn't want to be up the whole night before my graduation. Finally, I called some of the younger boys who were around, and the one or two others who were sober.

'I know how to slaughter. You, hold here. You, hold there,' I said, instructing them to help me so we could get on with it.

One of the kids involved told me later that it was one of the most shocking experiences of his life, as he had never before seen a woman involved in slaughtering a sheep. For me, taking action had nothing to do with being a man or a woman; you just did what you needed to. In my naive way I honestly didn't think there were things that I could not do as a woman. Yet here I was, suddenly feeling like my entire identity had come down to being someone else's wife or mother. I knew I needed more.

PART 2

◇◇◇◇◇◇◇◇◇◇◇◇◇◇

STEPPING OUT

When we commit to a vision to do something that has never been done before, there is no way to know how to get there. We simply have to build the bridge as we walk on it.

ROBERT E. QUINN

From *Building the Bridge as You Walk On It: A Guide to Leading Change*

PART 2

STEPPING OUT

CHAPTER 4

◇◇◇◇◇◇◇◇◇◇◇◇◇◇◇

Liberations

Scanning the Sunday paper classified ads one morning in March 1990, I came across a notice from Woolworths, announcing that they were accepting applications for their Graduate Trainee Programme. Training university graduates to become managers in retail since the 1980s, the Woolworths programme was extremely well regarded.

The fact was that a job in retail did not seem even remotely related to clinical psychology; nonetheless I figured my experience from my mother's shop might help me make the cut. If I got in, I could complete the programme and perhaps end up in human resources, where I would pick up some of that working-world 'life experience' that I lacked, and then qualify to do my Master's in clinical psychology in a few years' time. I applied through an agency and was called in for two interviews. In July that year I received the news that I had been accepted.

Our 1990 cohort was the first in the programme's history to include black graduates. Woolworths (still part of the Wooltru Group at the time) had always been a progressive company, and with Nelson Mandela recently released from prison and the ANC unbanned, its leadership, like many business leaders, had seen the writing on the wall. The company approached the country's transformation as an opportunity to excel in new ways, and our trainee group represented its first concrete effort to address the need for diversity in management.

While my decision to participate in the two-year programme meant moving from Alice to Cape Town, Presto supported my decision. In fact, he always encouraged my professional aspirations – first with my studies and now with my career. From a relatively poor family himself, he used to say that with my privileged upbringing and the great school I had attended, I had a responsibility to 'get out there' and make something of those advantages. He was also an incredibly loving and involved father – I used to joke that he had more maternal instincts than I initially did; my parenting strengths only emerged a bit later. With Presto's post at the University of Fort Hare and our home and community located in Alice, we decided I would go to Cape Town on my own, leaving nine-month-old Phila with his father. I would commute fortnightly by bus or minibus taxi to see them.

This arrangement seemed perfectly logical at the time, but looking back, I am keenly aware of how essential a supportive partner is to anyone with serious career ambitions. I don't know if women can ever 'have it all' in the sense of finding a stable balance between professional success and family life – personally, it has always been more of a juggling than balancing act. However you may view it, a reliable and trustworthy support network is absolutely vital to working parents, regardless of the 'level' at which you operate.

◇◇◇◇◇

Moving to Cape Town on my own was a real 'stepping out' for me. I had lived such a sheltered life, having always been under someone else's wing and protection: first my mother's watchful eye after my father's passing, then at a strict Seventh-Day Adventist boarding school, thereafter with my husband, whom I met early on in university. Eager to get the 'life experience' that Rhodes had insisted was required, I found myself energised by my independence and the opportunity to again apply my mind and will to something other than a crying baby. My son has been and remains the greatest joy and pride of my life, but looking back, I think those early months may have been clouded with post-partum depression, though I didn't have the term for it back then.

In contrast to Presto, my mother was not impressed by my decision to go and work in Cape Town. 'Do you mean to tell me that after all these years of studying psychology you now want to be a shopkeeper? You might as well have come back to work with me in the shop here at home,' she said.

Though I knew she was partly joking, I detected her disappointment that I was moving more than 1 000 kilometres away. I would no longer be able to relieve her of some of her duties in running the shop, something I had done regularly while I was in Alice, which was only 100 kilometres from Stutterheim. Also, as her firstborn child, I had been there for her since she was widowed, and she now felt abandoned. I realised then that it had never occurred to her that I might not see her business – which she had run so successfully and which had paid for me and so many others to get through university and more – as such an attractive proposition. In spite of my desire for more in life, I found my mother's belief in herself and the value of what she had built inspiring.

For many reasons then – and owing to the fact that we were the first black cohort, and because I was my mother's daughter – I took the Woolworths training programme experience and myself seriously. I didn't think there was anything unusual about my attitude until the first day of our induction. We all sat around a table while then CEO Syd Muller presented the vision and values session of the company. When he had finished, he asked our group of graduate trainees about our aspirations.

'I want to become a director at Woolworths,' I said when my turn came.

While I was at UNITRA, I had seen plenty of visible role models showing me that black people and women could be found at all strata of an organisation, so I found nothing exceptional about expressing this goal. After all, we were being asked about our aspirations.

The man facilitating the session, who was also black, nearly killed himself laughing.

'Why is that so funny?' I asked.

'There's not even a white woman on the board yet. Or a black man,' he said, looking at me in disbelief.

'Well, I guess there's an opportunity there,' I said, only this time not aloud, but as a mental note to myself.

Fifteen years later, in 2004, I was elated when Simon Susman invited me to join the Woolworths board as a non-executive director. From my mother's shop in Stutterheim to Woolworths head office in Cape Town I had come full circle as a retailer. My mother was proud.

'The University of Retail'

Woolworths' Graduate Training Programme was split into three streams: buying, merchandising and retail operations. I had been admitted as a buyer and I spent my first three months in stores (one month each in a small, medium and large store), learning everything from opening store procedures, to taking stock at the receiving bay, to maintaining the cold value chain for the food market. The second three months I worked with suppliers, learning how manufacturers organise their shop floors and factories, and absorbing all the detailed steps in a journey that begins when you place an order and concludes when that order gets out on the shop floor.

After the retail and supplier training, I spent twelve months at head office as part of a buying team in the Children's Wear department, under the direct supervision of my manager, Pam Davis. Looking back, I jokingly refer to this period as my 'Ugly Betty job' – as a junior buyer I helped the senior buyer to select a range of products, a job that sounds glamorous but included an unbelievable number of tasks (some very menial, and often on weekends or after hours), as well as smooth co-ordination, thorough research and sound instincts. Over the course of those eighteen months I was given various responsibilities from procuring fabric for other ranges to developing my own small range. The learning curve was steep.

For example, because children's clothes are often made from cotton, I spent time in different fabric mills where they wove cotton, especially denim, learning about different grades, how the dyeing works, and how long the process will take if you need 3 000 metres of a certain thickness dyed using a particular method. I needed that knowledge accurately to calculate the lead time necessary to place an order so that the correctly dyed fabric got to the manufacturer on time, and thus the final product – whose fabrication also incorporated considerations like ornamentation and practical concerns (for example, zippers versus buttons depending on the age of the child) – arrived on our shelves for the correct season.

The training we received constituted the most comprehensive and detailed programme of its kind in corporate South Africa, hence its nickname: 'the University of Retail'. The breadth and depth of the hands-on experience was incredible. It was also very intense and demanding, and at times required you to do things you didn't love (like ironing samples to prepare for a presentation or photographing competitors' clothes as part of marketing research). I learned so much in that programme, including the important truth that regardless of your academic degree, everyone starts somewhere. There will always be annoying aspects to any job, particularly in those early stages of your career, and you should view it all as part of a valuable learning experience of the bigger journey.

⋄⋄⋄⋄⋄

At Woolworths I found myself in a very high-performance culture anchored in quality. A whole value system had been built around this expectation of quality: attention to detail, never compromising on quality outcomes, and taking pride in everything you did. Related to the value of taking pride in everything was the organisational goal of being the best in the industry and even the world. Good was never good enough – we wanted to be best.

Woolworths was where I learned what a values-based organisation is all about. I came to understand that the company's values – in this case anchored in this notion of quality – are its DNA. A stamp that marked everything we did, from the quality of our products to the way we engaged with customers and suppliers, the whole organisation lived its values. As an employee, you felt this immediately when you walked into the wood-panelled head office which, with its open-plan layout, 'pause areas', hairdresser and ATM, was very modern for the time, while also exuding an aura of timeless elegance and quality. As a customer entering a Woolworths shop, you similarly experienced an environment of excellence, created by the warmth and professionalism of the people and the look and feel of the physical details.

From the moment I arrived in 1990, I found Woolworths such an exciting space to be part of. I thought I knew retail from having grown up in my mother's shop, but suddenly I was learning the science of retail. It was such a revelation for me to see how an organisation can choose what its defining hallmark will be, and then manifest that quality. How conscientious choices behind everything from how staff are treated to how media campaigns are run to the fabric of the salespeople's uniforms create an ambience or energy that both reflects and is mirrored back in a place, its people, and its leaders.

Small steps towards change

Right from the beginning, my position in Cape Town as a black African trainee manager brought a lot of personal growth. My very first appointment as a trainee was to the Woolworths store in Wynberg, a store where the sales assistants were mostly, if not all, coloured and where a black person had never been part of the management team, even as a trainee. The staff clearly didn't know what to make of me, but their bemusement was mostly of the innocent and curious variety given the historical context.

One afternoon I was in the staff canteen when one of the ladies from a group sitting together speaking in Afrikaans suddenly turned to me and asked in English if I knew what a microwave was. When I confirmed that I did, the woman told me they had been talking about a sale taking place at OK Stoves, an appliance shop across the road.

'You're a trainee manager, can't you afford one of these?' the woman asked, pointing to a flyer advertising the microwaves on sale.

'Sure, but I already have one,' I replied.

'You have a microwave oven?' she exclaimed. '*Jy lieg!*' Then she asked me to indicate which model I owned from those pictured in the flyer.

By chance the one I had, I think it was a Salton, was there, priced at something like R699.

'No! It's not possible,' she said in disbelief.

'Really, we do,' I said. 'My husband is a lecturer at a university,' I added, to give credence to my claim.

Translating our exchange to the other ladies, the woman said they wanted me to go to the shop with them the following day during our lunch break so that I could show them 'my' microwave oven.

Although it was the result of pure lack of exposure and not malice, these were the kinds of things I had to deal with all the time.

◇◇◇◇◇

There were also racial incidents that were not so innocent. More than once when I was at the customer service counter, white customers would see me and demand to speak to a manager, not accepting that I was that person.

Normally I could handle the situation. One day, however, a customer simply refused to talk to me, making it clear that a black manager was not acceptable. Seeing how put out she was, I offered to call our head office, something that was still occasionally done back then. We put her through to our head of Retail Operations at the time, Simon Susman, who later became CEO and is chairman of the board today.

'Ma'am, with the greatest respect, we'd really appreciate it if you would stop shopping at Woolworths. That person you're talking about is one of our staff members, and this is how things are,' Simon said after the woman had shared her grievance over not finding a white manager at the store.

She was so shocked. As was I. While I had been struggling to believe that someone felt so strongly about me being black that she refused to let me assist her, now I was equally astonished to see that someone else who was white felt so strongly about my right to do my job that he was prepared to tell a customer we didn't need her business.

Woolworths' cardinal rule has always been that the customer is always right. Simon's response was a clear message to the whole Woolworths system – both customers and employees who saw or would later hear about this incident – that when it came to ensuring that Woolworths black colleagues were treated as part of the company, the customer was not always right.

This was one of my first direct racial confrontations, and it opened my eyes to the fact that white people committed to treating people fairly and equally regardless of race also existed. It also demonstrated the power business leaders could wield when they clearly decided to change the status quo and were willing to say that certain behaviour was no longer acceptable. Those years at Woolworths in Cape Town showed me how an organisation or business can be a microcosm of what is happening in the larger society, and how whatever is happening externally plays back in the workplace.

⋄⋄⋄⋄⋄

There were about eight black people in our trainee peer group of 30, and the relationship between white and black trainees was collegial and supportive. In fact, it was because of our familiarity as a group that differences in the way we were incorporated into the company came to light. Over time numerous revelations were made, from the fact that all the black trainees had tertiary degrees while the same minimum requirement did not seem to have been applied to our white counterparts, to company policies that affected us but about which we were deliberately not informed.

One of the first examples that came up was around the costs trainees had incurred in relocating to Cape Town from other parts of the country. One day the black trainees were sharing experiences when a woman mentioned that some of her things had been damaged and broken in her move. She explained that she couldn't afford a removal truck, and so had been forced to load her furniture onto a bus.

'But why didn't the company pay for your move?' I asked, having recently learned about the company's 'relocation policy' from some of our white colleagues.

I had been sitting with a group of white colleagues a few weeks earlier when someone had expressed concern about her dog, which was being flown into Cape Town. Astonished that she could afford to fly her dog, I had asked for more details, only to discover that the company policy was to cover all relocation costs for the trainees, including your family's flights (and pets), a removal company, and a hotel for two weeks.

I shared this information with my black colleagues and when we realised that none of us had been informed of or benefited from this policy; we agreed that three of us would go to management to raise the issue. I had assumed that I had missed hearing about the 'relocation policy' because I had yet to move all my things from Alice.

We spoke to Dave van Eeden, director of HR at the time, who seemed genuinely surprised by the oversight. Dave followed up with the recruitment people who should have informed us about such things, asking why the policy had not been shared. Although we received apologies and reimbursements for the costs of our relocations, we never did get a 'reason' for what happened.

In a not dissimilar incident, there was a trip scheduled for the buyers' group to visit a fabric supplier in East London. Everything in the trainee programme was scheduled in advance, and so a week or so before the trip, having received no updates from HR, I went to ask for the details. The woman I spoke to in HR (the same recruitment person who had failed to inform the black trainees about the relocation policy) told me the trip was cancelled.

The following week one of my white trainee friends asked why I hadn't gone on the trip.

'I was told that trip was no longer happening,' I said.

'No, we were all there. I don't understand. You are part of our group, you should have been there,' she said.

I went back to HR, where the same recruitment woman claimed that she had been told the department budget could only accommodate so many trainees, which was why I had been cut. I then went to my divisional manager, who denied the existence of any such budget issue, adding that HR had never contacted him.

These episodes illustrated the fact that while the company was saying its vision and strategy and intent were to transform and embrace and support diversity, from a practical implementation and execution perspective, certain individuals were still operating according to their own rules.

There were numerous lessons that came out of this. First, it was clear that it was up to us to maintain a watchful eye and continually challenge every such instance that arose. In other words, if we found something had fallen through the cracks and chased it down only to receive answers or responses that were unacceptable, we would need to start questioning the company's commitment to diversity, and more importantly, its values at the leadership level. Time and again I have seen how it is the leaders who will set the tone for a company by driving the culture and living the values that influence and shape the thinking and processes in an organisation. Fortunately, when we raised these issues, Woolworths leadership acted swiftly to correct the situation, proving its commitment to its stated values.

The second lesson was around how you respond to such incidents. Instead of allowing myself to waste energy in outrage, I channelled it into gathering the facts, talking to other black colleagues and trainees to find out if what had happened was an isolated incident or part of a pattern. Through these discussions, it became clear that while the exclusion of black employees was a deliberate move on the part of certain people, it was also evident that our leaders and those at the higher levels of management were unaware that this was happening. Thus it was our responsibility to inform our managers when these sorts of things happened, because leaders cannot change things they do not know about. The point is, you cannot throw your toys out of the cot if the person making decisions is genuinely unaware of the situation; and the only way to create that awareness is by confronting such situations. Instead of focusing on our anger, we worked on fixing the problem. My constant refrain was, 'Seeing that we are your pilot group, here are some challenges that we keep facing, and we're not sure whether it's your policy or not.'

The final lesson from these incidents was around the way companies deal with individuals who resist change or reject company values. Proving that she was not aligned with the company's values, that woman in recruitment had made a career-limiting move; she went no further in the organisation. Often people like this will not necessarily be dismissed, but their career will stall when leadership realises they are not with the programme and have not bought into the value system or vision that leadership is trying to instil. When these kinds of incidents occur, people frequently complain that 'nothing' has happened to the person – I've heard this at every organisation I've worked. But how do they know nothing has happened? Typically you will not see a person asked to leave unless they were blatantly discriminating. Subtle discrimination – that is, people interpreting the rules in the way that suits them and their agendas – is difficult to pick up and even harder to fire someone for. So, although a person may not leave, I know that they will go no further in that company.

◇◇◇◇◇

As the first group of black trainees at Woolworths it was inevitable that we would face discrimination within the company. Fortunately, we found a supportive ally in Woolworths' HR director, Dave van Eeden. A big guy with a warm smile, Dave either fixed the issue or spoke to whoever could fix it. One day Dave invited a few of us to a meeting where he asked us to compile all the information that we could about the key challenges we faced as black employees, and the aspects of transformation that were not yet working. As the meeting closed, Dave asked me to stay behind.

'Tell me, how much do you like your job?' he asked.

'I like it very much,' I said.

'And how much do you like your car?' he said.

'Quite a lot,' I replied, wondering where this was going.

'I believe you are raising fundamental issues around some of the culture problems in the organisation. The board and top management are making decisions to change things, but people still don't change,' Dave began. He went on to explain that although he had shared these concerns with the board, some members still dismissed them as 'just HR' complaining.

'It would be good for the board to hear directly from you about your experiences,' he said.

He then asked me to identify a few colleagues among the black trainees and lead a presentation to the board about the challenges we as black professionals faced in the company. 'Would you do that?' he asked, warning me that this was the kind of presentation that could be career limiting if it did not go well. His questions about how much I liked my job and car were posed so as to be clear about what was at stake, should I commit to raising these issues in front of the board.

I was in. About three weeks later five of us, one of whom was Joe Mwase, went to meet the board. We had put together a thorough presentation, having spoken with colleagues across the Western Cape to present a well-structured and comprehensive picture. In essence what we were saying was that the company claimed to want to give us the opportunity to develop, but inconsistent or belated access to information about opportunities – from housing policies to courses and seminars – hindered our ability to develop equally.

I still remember the feeling of intimidation when I walked into that boardroom, where nearly a dozen white male directors sat around a huge oval table. While one of our colleagues prepared the projector and transparencies (yes, this was life pre-PowerPoint), another colleague suddenly started apologising profusely to the board, distancing himself from the presentation to come. He began by saying, 'You mustn't think we aren't grateful for the opportunity of working for this company ...' As he continued to babble in this vein, the rest of us listened, shocked, wondering where this was coming from. Finally, Joe Mwase interrupted him, saying, 'You are not representing us, or me, and these viewpoints are out of order.'

After this unfortunate false start, we gave our presentation. The board was receptive and curious, asking numerous questions for clarity. They thanked us at the end, and not long afterwards interventions to address our concerns manifested.

Among the issues we raised was that of the inhospitable reception we received as black people arriving to the Western Cape in the early 90s from other provinces: in so many ways, we felt we had entered a space we were not supposed to be. For example, finding decent centrally located accommodation through the usual channels had proved impossible for most of us. 'Sorry, it's already taken' was the inevitable response as soon as the person on the other end of the line heard your accent or surname. As a result, many of the black trainees lived in shared accommodation far from the city centre (I spent my first six months in Cape Town sharing a flat with my husband's cousin in Gugulethu).

Recognising our predicament and that there was little we or they could do to force the larger society to change in that moment, one of the company's concrete responses to our presentation was the purchase of six flats in the Cape Technicon (District 6) and Gardens neighbourhoods for the black trainees to rent. When those filled up, the company rented additional flats in Woolworths' name, sub-leasing them to black employees as needed.

The lesson here is that if a company is committed to making change, it will invest in the necessary provisions and support to enable that change to happen both within *and* outside the company. But again, that level of commitment can only come from an organisation's leaders and decision-makers. Without that visible commitment, which is manifested in resourcing the right interventions, change will not happen. And even then, because individuals will still hold their personal views, constant follow-up and monitoring are necessary. Unfortunately, this latter point remains true even today.

The second lesson from this experience was that when you speak truth to power, you need to know that your truth is based on principles that are clearly articulated in your own mind. You also have to understand that when raising serious or contentious issues, the response may not be what you expect or desire, and if things go south, you must be ready to stand by your viewpoint, regardless of what others will say or do. That day I also learned never to go into a meeting with someone whom you do not trust is coming from the same perspective as yours. In distancing himself from us, what our colleague who got cold feet was in fact demonstrating his fear and concern for his job, something that Dave van Eeden had indirectly asked me when earlier briefing me about this presentation ('How much do you like your car?'). One lesson to take away, though, if you find yourself in a situation like that and things go awry, is that above all you need to be able to stand up for the principle behind your truth. Fortunately, in Joe I had found a kindred spirit, and over the years we both went on to partner as leaders within the BMF Western Cape. I could go to 'war' with Joe.

The final lesson from all of this was around the power of networks. As black trainees we initially engaged informally in a 'network' that started as several of us sitting together in the canteen. This led to socialising after hours and more introductions to each other. It was thanks to that informal network that we discovered things like the inconsistency in the relocation policy. When we started engaging with management about these issues, the network became formal. Formalising the network was key to change, as it was ultimately what got us in front of the board, which in turn resulted in raising leadership's awareness about ways that the Cape Town environment was not ready to embrace black people – something that could then be addressed in the form of actions like securing appropriate housing and reimbursing our relocations.

Learning to lead

Eighteen months after arriving in Cape Town, I had achieved my training programme goal of managing my own department. For two years I was in charge of buying for the Children's Outerwear department (ages 12–36 months). Although it was a tremendous learning experience, I knew this was not what I wanted to do with my life.

During that time I continued to be a relatively frequent visitor to Dave van Eeden's office, generally coming with concerns about unequal treatment, and always with my dog-eared copy of the Woolworths' *Vision and Values* booklet and a firm belief that the company wanted to do the right thing. It was because of this that in May 1993 Dave van Eeden invited me to move to HR to join the Training and Development department, where I would help review the company's new diversity culture programme under Kim Watson. One of the company's few female senior managers, Kim was a smart, assertive UCT business school MBA graduate and a progressive leader in the HR development space. Intense, confident, and comfortable in herself, Kim was also an ideas person; she would often invite you to join her outside to discuss her latest insight as she 'caught a smoke'.

Based on the experiences of our trainee cohort as well as other black colleagues, I helped design the diversity culture programme module, which was part of Woolworths' broader training programme to help staff better understand and handle issues around diversity and transformation. In those days much of the material was very basic stuff around dealing with people's cultural differences – for example, explaining why black people shook hands with a 'limp' rather than 'firm' grip, or did not look people in the eye when speaking (both the result of different cultural norms around what is polite and respectful) – this in contrast to diversity and inclusion programmes of recent times, where deep issues of unconscious bias, among others, are explored. The module we designed gave staff a platform to discuss issues like the fact that all the signage in our stores was printed only in English and Afrikaans, and that African languages were exclusively used for signs explaining that management did not have the keys to the safe or that there were no jobs available. In the main, we were trying to bust the seriously patronising myths that were the narrative of the day regarding black people.

Because developing the module was not a full-time job, Dave also asked me to take on the new full-time position of Community Affairs manager.

Although the Wooltru Group, of which Woolworths was a part, had a budget for social responsibility projects, there was no real framework, focus, or even a dedicated manager at the group level. An ad hoc committee composed of a changing roster of people decided how to use the funds, which were then administered through Wooltru's HR.

With a mandate to develop Woolworths' own direct interface for a corporate social responsibility (CSR) programme, my first job was to design our strategy and focus areas. This meant determining which community organisations Woolworths would become involved with, how we should get involved, and how we would disperse funds. In my career I have been particularly fortunate to come into almost all of my jobs at points in time when they were practically blank canvases, allowing me to define the role, shape the strategy and determine how the role or programme or division fitted into the rest of the organisation. Essentially it was a greenfield situation, where I had a lot of latitude to conceive what the position was and to co-create with others what the end state should look like.

Coming in to create Woolworths' CSR programme, I was given a budget, a secretary and three boxes of letters that had been sitting in a corner of Kim Watson's office. With the help of my secretary, Eunice Lubbe, the first thing I did was go through those letters, which were applications for funding from various communities across the country. Next I began a benchmarking exercise, reviewing annual reports from other well-developed social responsibility programmes, studying their frameworks, what they were doing, and how much they were spending. Combining that knowledge with an examination of the areas of need across the country, I targeted three core areas: education, the environment and job creation. Then I developed a strategic framework for Woolworths to establish the systems and processes of a CSR programme focused on those core areas of 'the 3 Ps': people, planet and profits.

To augment our relatively limited CSR funds, I initiated an employee volunteering programme. Creating community affairs committees in each division and/or store, employees identified community projects that addressed at least one of the three focus areas; they then adopted a project, for which they raised funds. Matching rand for rand, whatever the committee raised, we leveraged our CSR programme to get colleagues working together as teams, creating more internal cohesion while also getting our staff to engage externally with what was happening in the communities around them, all while raising funds for worthy projects. Much fun was had by all, and with the teams raising thousands of rand through creative campaigns, the programme became a flagship, especially at head office.

⋄⋄⋄⋄⋄

As I progressed up the ladder, I found myself increasingly in a position where I needed to uphold the organisation's values. This was easy to do because the highest leadership at Woolworths consistently did the same. Colin Hall was chairman of the board during the period when I worked for HR in Training and Development through to the time when I moved to Corporate Affairs. Placing a huge emphasis on values, Colin actively used his role as chairman to promote his insights about our 'shared' African values, traditions and languages.

To pull us together as South Africans doing our part in nation-building, Colin continually encouraged everyone in the organisation to demonstrate the value of Ubuntu, the African concept that proclaims 'I am what I am because of who we all are'. He also liked to invoke 'Seriti', a Sotho concept that translates as 'shadow' but carries a much deeper meaning based on the understanding that each person casts a unique shadow and the importance of acknowledging others for who they are. The closest English translation would be 'dignity' or 'integrity', though neither word fully captures the idea.

It was incredibly powerful to see the chairman of a company like Woolworths using that language and context and narrative at that time. Colin was a key thought leader in the country and an influencer in society, and his choice to promote African values in this way among his peer group demonstrated how a top leader can use his networks to change society at different levels.

A big fan of Stephen Covey's *The 7 Habits of Highly Effective People*, Colin had purchased the rights to run Covey workshops in South Africa. Most of us in HR, myself included, became master trainers of the Covey Program, facilitating free workshops in the company and for the community leaders and school principals with whom we had relationships through our CSR engagements. Through those engagements we had the pleasure of working with a school principal by the name of Mr Al Witten, headmaster of Zerilda Park Primary School in Lavender Hill, Retreat. Two years after our work together, Al decided to further his studies on school administration and leadership. Winning a scholarship, he completed his PhD at Harvard University in the USA. Years later he returned to South Africa as a guest of the Human Resource Development Council's (HRDC) chair, then deputy president of South Africa, Dr Phumzile Mlambo-Ngcuka, who had committed to work with school principals in the country.

CHAPTER 5

◇◇◇◇◇◇◇◇◇◇◇◇◇◇

Embracing democracy

By 1993, politically and socially the mood in the country – and as we felt it in Cape Town – was palpably changing. As South Africa hurtled towards the first democratic elections, set for April 1994, Cape Town-based organisations from the City of Cape Town to the big oil and insurance companies were all recruiting black professionals, and a vibrant black community was growing in the business, political and social spaces. It was during one of the many discussions we held as black colleagues about the progress Woolworths was (and was not) making that someone suggested we should join the Black Management Forum (BMF) – Joe Mwase brought us the membership forms.

Founded in 1976, the BMF was established as a non-racial organisation to support and develop management and leadership among black professionals. I began attending meetings in late 1993, and right from the start I found the open discussions and debates about the challenges black people faced at work refreshing and robust. After attending for about six months, I decided to pay my membership fees and become an active member. Unlike the other black professional organisations, the BMF is not specific to any one profession,[1] and has consistently had members from across different professions and areas of management.

In its first decade the BMF focused on transformation issues in South

African offices of multinational companies. Facing increasing pressure from head offices, multinationals operating in apartheid South Africa were increasingly compelled to follow the US-based Sullivan Code of Principles, which dictated that they have affirmative action programmes in place to hire black employees, some of whom should be in management. As a result of this, a few black managers could be found, mainly in Gauteng.

Coming together to form the BMF, these individuals – including founder Eric Mafuna, who worked in advertising at the time – focused the organisation on the challenges black professionals faced when navigating the corporate world, particularly looking at issues around getting the necessary recognition and support in that environment. The BMF's original vision was to create a talent pool of black professionals at management levels, and developing access to opportunities was a primary concern. Over the years, the BMF, an organisation of black intelligentsia, became increasingly national in scope as different multinationals like Shell, Caltex, Nestle, and Unilever employed more black managers in cities beyond Johannesburg.

In the mid-1980s the BMF began engagements with the ANC, which at the time was operating in exile from Lusaka, Zambia. While working for political justice and emancipation was obviously critical, BMF leaders recognised the need to also understand what an economic justice and emancipation programme would look like. Discussions with the ANC focused around how the ANC saw economic transformation unfolding in the country upon its return from exile, and how the BMF could help define an ideology for black management and leadership that was aligned with the ANC's non-racial, non-sexist values, as well as to the Freedom Charter, which views the economy as belonging to all the people.

The BMF's thinking complemented the ANC's vision of economic transformation, even though the ANC's concern would remain aligned with unions. The ANC also recognised that black managers had a key role to play in the transformation of the economy. When the ANC was unbanned and returned to South Africa in the early 90s, that complementary relationship continued, resulting in the ANC later inviting the BMF to play a role in formulating the country's transformation laws as part of the National Economic Development and Labour Council (NEDLAC) negotiations.[2]

As a BMF member in those heady days, I got to participate in the BMF's internal discussions around economic transformation. It was like taking a crash course on the issues of economic transformation, opening my eyes to what had happened in our country historically and what needed to happen going forward. We were on the verge of achieving political freedom, but the question of economic transformation – and how to obtain it – loomed large.

Participating in the BMF helped me understand the key levers that needed to be pulled to influence and shift economic power so that it no longer sat only in white hands. The BMF's view, which I very much took on, was that that shift lay in the vital issue of developing people, particularly within the professions and at management and leadership levels. As black people we were on the point of attaining political freedom and therefore accessing economic empowerment, but who would run our companies and how could we ensure that we effectively managed the nation's economy? These questions were at the core of the BMF's focus on managerial and leadership development: to prepare people to be in a position to take up the opportunities that would lead our country in the direction it ought to go.

The BMF consolidated the political awareness that had awoken in me years before when I learned about Jack and his corrupt vouchers: that moment when I realised that the apartheid system went so much deeper and was so much more layered than it appeared at first glance. I saw that to change the system, you needed to understand all the layers and levers. Employment equity, broader representation, and skills development were all key to ensuring that people had both the skills and training, and the chance to use those skills and training, to achieve their own economic empowerment. It was an incredibly exciting, powerful and influential time and it shaped and concentrated my political awareness and understanding.

PART 2: STEPPING OUT

When magic showed its face

On 27 April 1994 the country held its first democratic elections and the effect in Cape Town was profound – suddenly there was an ANC parliament and with it a whole new group of black decision-makers and politicians coming to debate and create our new democracy. For my own part, after voting in that historic election, I made a promise to contribute seriously to our society's reconstruction and development. I was filled with a renewed sense of purpose and a deep commitment to being part of the process to build the new South Africa.

I never guessed that my pledge would be called upon as soon as it was. About two weeks after the election we received a call from a family friend, Pops Mageza, with an 'urgent request'. Presto and Phila had relocated from Alice to Cape Town about a year after my arrival. After the first couple of years of staying in one of the company flats, we had in 1993 bought our own house in Thornton, a suburb in Goodwood.

I thought Pops wanted to speak to Presto, but he said he actually was calling me and kept referring to 'UMama'. For a few minutes I was confused. Not only was Pops not his usual jovial self, but he was whispering with a sense of urgency. Pops went on to explain that he was in a meeting in Mama's house with Peter Mokaba, who was ANC Youth League president at the time, and some others, and was acting on behalf of one of them. It turned out that the urgent request was for us to 'host' Mama Winnie Mandela when she came to Cape Town for the first democratic opening of parliament and swearing in of the MPs. Various controversies at the time meant that she was hounded by the media, and the people who asked us to host Mama Winnie wanted her location to remain private. I was in a state of shock and honoured excitement, not least because Mama Winnie was scheduled to arrive the following day at noon. All I could think was that my house was in no state to host someone of her stature.

'Not to worry, Litha, Mama is a very humble person,' Pops assured me. 'I've been to your house several times and trust your hospitality skills. I know she will be very happy with this arrangement.'

I put down the phone and immediately started cleaning my house – when

I left for the airport the next day to fetch Mama Winnie, Presto was still tidying up!

Cape Town International Airport was jam-packed with the new ANC MPs and their entourages arriving from all over the country. Emotionally overwhelmed by the sight of those faces, I burst into tears.

Only two days earlier, the Independent Electoral Commission (IEC) had announced the ANC's overwhelming majority victory. Now here I was, in the middle of what looked like an ANC Women's League victory party. And there stood Mama Winnie: tall, beautiful and smiling, talking to her ANCWL colleagues, Sis Thandi Modise next to her, and Mama Albertina Sisulu walking towards her, holding Mama Gertrude Shope's hand. It was a magical moment and it changed my life forever. In that period different people experienced different 'magical' moments, and for many it was voting. For me, that day at the airport was the first and most immediately tangible evidence I had that we were living in a new era, that political change had been achieved, and that I would be included in the new South Africa. What I had voted for a few weeks earlier suddenly became real.

One of Mama's bodyguards drove my car as we left the airport, turning me into part of the entourage as we headed straight to parliament. I spent the rest of the day running up and down, trying to help register everyone for the swearing in the following day. For most, if not all of the ANC MPs, it was the first time since the election results that they were all meeting in one place. I can only imagine that for many it was the moment of truth and relief: that what they and millions of others had been fighting for all these years had finally happened. Freedom in our lifetime. The next day the MPs were sworn in, nominating and then electing Nelson Mandela as the first president of the new Republic of South Africa.

◇◇◇◇◇

To my delight and honour, Mama Winnie's 'few nights' visit stretched into a 135-day stay at our home. Very much 'settled and at home', Mama refused to move to either the hotel or government house that had been made available to her, first as an MP and later as deputy minister of Science, Arts and Culture.

'Nkosazana, you can move to those big and cold houses built by the apartheid government. As for me I'm perfectly happy here in the warmth of my newfound family,' she replied when I asked when she might want to move. At the same time, the media was printing stories about Mama Winnie 'living large in a five-star Cape Town hotel at taxpayers' expenses'. Talk about fake news!

I suspect that the special attraction of our house was my son Phila, who was about four years old at the time. I think he was a proxy for her many grandchildren whom she missed terribly throughout her long stay in Cape Town. Every evening Mama spent at least an hour on the phone talking to them. One by one, she asked them about school and their friends, mediating any issues they were having. Nothing was too small for her to discuss with those little ones. Our telephone was in the dining room, and we often ended up giggling while listening to a song from one child and then a school play rehearsal from another. I learned so much from her about being fully present when engaging with children: just one of the many valuable lessons Mama Winnie taught me.

As the deputy minister of Arts, Science and Culture, Mam Winnie often was with her team late into the evenings planning for the next day. Regardless of the hour, she always knocked at our door to inform us of her whereabouts for the next day. I would answer, often in my nightgown, and we inevitably would end up in a long conversation about one of the many fascinating subjects within her portfolio. Her knowledge and diligence amazed me.

I was working as Woolworths' Community Affairs manager at the time, and those talks with Mama deepened my understanding of how to match corporate social responsibility strategy with real community needs to achieve meaningful and lasting impact. This was done first and foremost by going into a community not to impose your preconceived ideas about what it required, but rather doing proper research and choosing projects that met real needs based on community consultation.

Mama's background in social work also helped me refine my approach to community consultation when defining and articulating needs. Because 'community' is such a broad label – so many people make up any community, and those people may not see needs similarly – it was essential that we engage with as many different people in the community as possible to verify and confirm what was really the most pressing need according to a majority of interests.

'Don't you want to go and visit your projects in Gugulethu? You want to be sure that your company has not ended up wasting money on a white elephant,' she'd say to me on weekends when she was around. At the time there were so many projects sponsored or donated by companies – things like libraries built simply because there had not been one before.

But I also knew better than to fall for Mama's attempts to make an unannounced trip to the township free of her entourage. We were under strict instructions from her staff and Peter Mokaba not to let her go anywhere without her bodyguards. Although Mama was seen by the majority of people as our Mother of the Nation, many white Capetonians saw her as 'that woman' who challenged and scared people with her uncompromising statements and actions.

While we tried to keep Mama's presence a secret, my neighbours eventually discovered the identity of our houseguest. One day the mother of my son's best friend across the road was dropping Phila at home and asked if she could come in to say hello to my mother.

'But my mother is not here,' I said.

'No, Phila said his grandmother is visiting,' my neighbour, who had met my mother previously, insisted.

The next thing I knew, I saw Mama emerging from the passage saying, 'Is that my grandchild?' and coming straight to the door.

My neighbour's face went red at the sight of Mama.

'What is this woman doing in your house?' she asked, grabbing her son and making her way across the road before I could even respond.

PART 2: STEPPING OUT

Ten minutes later she rang the bell again, informing me that it was 'irresponsible' to keep Mama Winnie in my house with my child.

We were close because of the kids, but there was a chill on our relationship for some weeks after that. A month or so later *You* magazine published a story claiming that Winnie Mandela was staying in a fancy hotel with her entourage, spending taxpayers' money, etc. I took it over to my neighbour, making the point that she shouldn't believe everything she read. She apologised, we made peace, and I suggested that the kids could play at her house if that made her feel better.

◇◇◇◇◇

There will always be a lot of lessons for all of us around the life of Winnie Mandela and how society and history treated her over the years. For me one of the biggest takeaways from her life was how she handled herself as a leader, never showing in public how that treatment got to her. When you go through negative public situations as she did, people either expect you to hide your face or, when you are out there, to look bowed down. But Winnie's head was always held high. She was there to do her business. It takes courage to walk out into situations knowing what's being said about you but continuing to focus on your goal. Notably as a leader, your job is to maintain focus and push your goal forward, regardless of what else is going on or who is there or not there to support you: you stand tall and strong because you know you are advancing a principle you believe in.

In later years when I was driving the transformation agenda and fighting for the voiceless – speaking up for race and gender transformation in boardrooms – I would remember Mama Winnie's advice: 'It's better to piss inside the tent than sit outside where you'll have little chance to change anything!' That had been her response when, in my relative naivety, I had asked why she was letting people treat her the way they did. She explained that she was a member of the ANC, she had earned her place inside, and she was going to use it to change things from within. The message was to stay the course, not allow yourself to become distracted from your goal, be tenacious as a leader, but also not to lose your sense of humour. That woman had a great and wicked sense of humour.

Finally, the way Mam Winnie modelled how to be present with children really helped my parenting attitude at the time. No matter how tired she was, she made time to tend to the connection with her grandchildren. As a young working mother, I learned from her that regardless of my busy schedule, weekends with my son had to be quality time. This meant making sure that we weren't just in the room together, but having conversations and actively engaging. Fortunately, Cape Town was a great environment to raise a child, and to this day I cherish those times with my son driving to Table Mountain, going for walks, or picnicking on a beach or at Kirstenbosch Gardens.

My Cape Town

In many ways Cape Town was where I genuinely experienced full growth intellectually, emotionally and politically. When I look back, I see how my previous years set me on a path, but it was in Cape Town that that path started to lead somewhere I wanted to go. That said, I also knew that my experience of Cape Town was not typical for black people, especially when it came to those of us not originally from the city.

One of the challenging aspects of that time in the 90s in Cape Town was seeing how overwhelming the changes were for some black Africans from the Western Cape, a place where the apartheid government had very successfully played races against one another, leaving black Africans always at the bottom. You could feel the confusion over the black people now coming from outside the Western Cape, 'jumping in' and taking jobs that had never been open to black Capetonians because they were African rather than so-called coloured.

This was illustrated to me one afternoon at the canteen in Woolworths' head office. One of the aunties who had worked in the canteen as long as I could remember was there that day, speaking to a black professional whom I knew from outside Woolworths. He was on his way out, and I went over to greet him. I asked him what he was doing there.

'I was here to visit my mother,' he replied in Xhosa.

I then realised he was talking about that auntie, whom I had always thought of as coloured, and who had never spoken Xhosa to me.

Returning to the canteen, I went to her and said, 'I didn't know you were so-and-so's mother?' Her mouth just dropped.

'Please don't say anything to anyone,' she said. 'It was so difficult to get this job.'

Like many black Africans who could, she had conducted herself as a coloured person because the reality in the Western Cape was that such pretence made it easier to get a job. There were many stories like this, and they spoke volumes about the troubles people faced. They were also good reminders of the fact that we all come from different backgrounds – socially, politically, economically – and that the experience of being black can never be reduced to one 'common' experience. At the BMF we often spoke about the depth and breadth of the black experience, and how all those different histories had to be respected and acknowledged.

CHAPTER 6

Earning a place at the table

With the heat being turned up on the debates around South Africa's affirmative action legislation, I redoubled my commitment to our country's restructuring, becoming increasingly active and vocal in the BMF's Cape Town branch.

At that time our regional chair, Gavin Pietersen, was pushing for the Western Cape to host the organisation's 1997 annual conference. However, with our one branch, the national office told us that we could not compete with the Gauteng and KZN regions. To be a serious contender we would have to increase the number of BMF branches and members, initiate more active programmes that our members saw value in, and influence the national discourse through robust debates on the policy issues related to the BMF's vision of transformation and leadership development.

We got to work right away, so much so that between 1994 and 1996 we tripled our membership and opened several branches, including one in Rondebosch, which I opened and chaired. As BMF Rondebosch chair, my duties were to grow the new branch's membership, hold regular forums on critical topics with key speakers addressing our members, and host relevant workshops on transformation and leadership development.

PART 2: STEPPING OUT

'Suitably qualified'

A key BMF issue during this time was around defining and including a 'suitably qualified' clause in the Employment Equity legislation, which was still being discussed as a white paper. How to define whether or not someone was 'suitably qualified' for a position was a key question that we as the BMF wanted to have clearly resolved in the legislation.

The BMF position was that the requirements for suitable qualification had to be clear and specific, with different jobs reflecting different qualifications. In particular we wanted to ensure that industry experience and recognition of prior learning could substitute for a four-year degree where appropriate. For this to function, we needed a transparent framework to assess a person's qualifications and experience in a credible and objective way. This is where the National Qualifications Framework (NQF) was developed as part of the Skills Development Act, so that institutions had a recognised framework to measure and validate prior learning as a qualification.

As the BMF we ran workshops and gathered information, bringing people in to discuss these concepts and then developing a clause (to add to the Employment Equity white paper) which expressed our position. We seconded BMF North West regional chair Mzwanele Manyi[3] to lobby together with labour unions (specifically COSATU within NEDLAC) to get that clause pushed through and accepted as part of the Employment Equity Act of 1997.

Because of this, the Employment Equity Act of 1997 (which includes the clause defining 'suitably qualified') and the Skills Development Act of 1998 (which includes the NQF) should be aligned to and speak to one another, and must be read in conjunction. Together, these acts reflected and underpinned the BMF's argument that you must skill people through different exposures, rotations and experiences to develop their readiness to take up positions as they arise, which in turn enables companies to meet their Employment Equity targets.

For me, participating in the process of developing a piece of legislation from white paper to green paper to law was a fascinating experience. The discussions that we as the BMF engaged in in parliament with different stakeholders, including the labour unions, also underscored the truth that we all come to these things with our own perspectives. I increasingly saw how people's different backgrounds resulted in radically different worldviews, reminding me again that there are as many experiences of being black in South Africa as there are black South Africans. My larger takeaway message was around the importance of consulting a wide array of stakeholders before making major decisions.

Meanwhile, getting my own voice into the conversations that were shaping the future of our country was a huge development experience and privilege, but it also came at a cost. By necessity our meetings were held after hours and on weekends, which made it difficult for me as a young mother with a child and family to be present in all these spheres. The year before I became branch chair, I had hired an au pair to take on some of the child care load. I also persuaded my mother to move from the Eastern Cape to help me with Phila, who by then was eight. My mother was at a stage in her life when she was ready to leave the Ngqika Store in the hands of my younger brother and to take a break from teaching. The new arrangement worked out well but nonetheless I often found myself bringing Phila with me to meetings, probably more frequently than he would have liked. Juggling my job at Woolworths and my responsibilities as branch chair with motherhood was very challenging for me at this point.

⋄⋄⋄⋄⋄

Back at Woolworths I was still working in Corporate Social Responsibility (under HR) when the company decided to create its own Corporate Affairs division. The company was preparing to leave the Wooltru Group and look to be listed independently on the JSE. Woolworths needed its own Corporate Affairs division to handle investor relations, external communications and corporate social responsibility. It also needed someone to run it.

I had been leading the CSR work under HR for about eighteen months by then. I asked Dave van Eeden what the new Corporate Affairs job would entail. Dave said that in addition to leading the company's CSR (which I was already doing), the position included functions like external communications and investor relations. It also entailed moving from HR to the Finance department, which was responsible for the listing process.

The next thing I knew, I was meeting with Woolworths' financial director, Ian Sturrock, for a kind of interview. I say 'kind of' because those internal interviews are not as much about your qualifications or accomplishments as they are about who you are and whether there is a culture fit. A few weeks later, in May 1996, Ian called to say I had got the job of head of Corporate Affairs. It was a big promotion, and like almost all the jobs I have had, it thrust me into a role that was new to the company and therefore in unchartered territory. I was encouraged to be as ambitious as possible.

Since I was developing something new, Ian gave me the time to think deeply around how I envisioned the role and to benchmark what was happening externally. I quickly saw that whether the role would be big or small was going to be a function both of my personal drive and aspirations, as well as external support. When I say support, I mean both moral support and the resources – the people, the space and the capacity – required. Both types of support were abundantly supplied.

This new role with Ian as my boss turned out to be the best of all worlds. The challenge of creating the role while being so well supported was an incredibly empowering experience. I had my own division with a much larger budget than I had had in CSR, and six rather than just two people reporting to me. I also had a new boss in Ian, who became my first real business mentor.

A tall and slender man with a gentlemanly bearing and a sharp mind, Ian was one of the first men I worked with whom I would describe as a feminist. He had two daughters, whom he adored and spoke of highly, and always treated women as complete equals. Exceptionally gender sensitive and empowering to the women he worked with, Ian mentored most of the company's senior women at one point or another. He was keenly aware of the fact that as a black woman rising up through the ranks, I was in the spotlight, and he wanted me to succeed. Because of this he was also tough on me.

'You know people think you'll get a soft pass. You don't want people to think that, so you've got to deliver and step up,' he would say very frankly.

When I joined his ExCo team, which consisted of six white men – all high-level finance managers responsible for key organisational functions – it quickly became clear that there were some among them who could not understand why I was present and being given equal time to discuss my portfolio, which a few of the finance people looked down on as 'just' communications.

'You've earned a place at the table, but it's up to you how you use it,' Ian said. 'You've got to own that space.'

That truth was made clear right from the beginning of those weekly ExCo meetings. At each of the first three meetings I attended, a certain colleague skipped over me when distributing his report. The first time when he said he was one short I wrote it off as an honest mistake – after all, I was new and could share with the person next to me.

The following week he again handed his report to everyone but me. This time I sat stewing, my mind filling with noise: calm down, this is not happening, this person doesn't mean what he's doing, maybe he forgot, maybe next time he'll remember that you are there, don't embarrass yourself by saying something. Consumed by my thoughts, the meeting was spoiled and I may as well not have been there.

The following week I was obviously ready. Once again he arrived one report short. As he was about to start the session, I interrupted.

'Sorry, I don't have a copy of the report,' I said to the meeting chair, who was Ian.

Someone offered to share theirs.

'No, I don't want to share. This is the third time this is happening. Either this person can't count, is saying I shouldn't see this report, or has an issue with me being part of this meeting,' I said.

The room went very quiet before Ian spoke.

'It's good that you brought this to my attention. Can we get to the next agenda item while so-and-so goes and makes a copy of the report for Nolitha so we can get going again?' Ian said, not missing a beat.

After the meeting Ian called me in. 'You handled that well. You don't fight and shout: you state the facts and that way we all get it,' he affirmed.

This incident reflected an important truth about organisations and values: when we say an organisation needs to be clear about what it stands for this really comes down to what kind of behaviour senior management allows. If your organisation is not clear about what it stands for and people are allowed to behave in a manner that isn't aligned with the purported values, that is the message you are sending, and you will employ and recruit the wrong people, thus creating the 'wrong' culture. This responsibility – to demonstrate what behaviour is tolerated and what is not, and what the 'face of success' looks like by whom you promote and support – sits with top leadership. For me at that time, Ian became the face of integrity in business.

◇◇◇◇◇

Not long after being appointed head of Corporate Affairs, I was sent to London. From September to November 1996, the Marks & Spencer Corporate Affairs team hosted me as I absorbed how international corporate affairs divisions of substance ran, both at Marks & Spencer and other London-based companies. This international benchmarking experience would help me set up Woolworths' Corporate Affairs division; it provided me with vital first-hand knowledge about the structure and strategy behind the communications space, including how to handle external media, investor relations and public relations. It was here that I began to practise the art of capturing the key message in any communication, and also came to grasp the importance of clearly articulating those key messages and ensuring consistency between internal (staff) and external (customers) messaging. Realising that consistency in messaging is key to communicating a brand, I also learned that your external brand image must carry back through to your employee value proposition. In other words, you cannot be good to your customers and bad to your employees or vice versa.

The trip to London was both my first time travelling abroad and the company's first instance of sending a black representative overseas. Woolworths had a long-standing and highly valued relationship with Marks & Spencer, and still does. The experience was incredibly validating on both personal and professional levels to be trusted in this capacity.

My stay in London offered a period of intense learning, but the thing that really touched and stayed with me was how curious people were about South Africa's '1994 miracle'. Two years into South Africa's democracy, my Marks & Spencer colleagues really wanted to understand how democracy was unfolding and how Mandela's government was engaging with business. I found myself constantly being asked where the country was going. Much as I enjoyed talking about South Africa and the opportunities for growth and development that I believed were abundant in our new democracy, I also worried about the extent to which I was sometimes cast in that uncomfortable role of speaking for black South Africans. Through this experience I also came to see how the world had become a global village, and that the feeling that 'everyone was watching' – which I had personally experienced as a black woman in boardrooms – extended to our entire country: the world was watching South Africa.

This trip also demonstrated the importance of international exposure as a career investment with a long-term payoff, something Ian reminded me about the following year when I submitted my annual budget.

'This is incomplete, you've got two lines missing in the budgeting scope,' he said, returning it to me.

'What do you mean?' I said, sure I had covered everything.

'The first line you're missing is for courses or seminars or conferences that you or your people will go on this year. And the second line is international travel. There's no way a senior manager of your stature should not be travelling internationally at least once a year,' he said.

And of course he was right. Attending international conferences and keeping abreast of global trends in one's industry are vital to remaining plugged in and at the top. Unfortunately, when times are tough, companies use discretion to cut back on training and development, especially when it comes to international travel, which is absolutely the wrong thing to do, as you are effectively scrapping an investment with long-term payoffs.

Ian's practice of always reminding me of the importance of my own and others' development was one of the real advantages of having a line manager who was also my mentor. I am glad to say it is something I immediately started paying forward, making sure to have the same 'development' conversations with my people.

The value of a mentor

A mentor can be many things to you in your career, but first and foremost, a mentor listens, acting as a sounding board for you to process decisions and arrive at your own conclusions. Besides the obvious personal growth and development that comes from sitting with someone whom you respect and look up to (professionally, as a leader, or spiritually), the one-on-one mentorship relationship is a unique opportunity to practise a level of vulnerability and honesty that can be otherwise scarce in competitive work environments.

When thinking of great personal mentors, I most often come back to my relationship with Ian Sturrock. In our initial conversations I remember being cautious about how much I would admit to him as my boss if I had fallen short on my targets. However, as our relationship shifted into the mentorship space, I dropped the façade. I knew that his input and feedback came from a desire to see me succeed. Making this transition and accepting unpleasant feedback was not always easy, however.

Ian had been my boss for about a year when I came up for promotion to senior manager (head of Corporate Affairs). I was in the lift one day when one of his colleagues entered and congratulated me. Seeing my puzzled expression, he explained how excited and proud the ExCo had been to support my promotion. He could see from the confusion that must have been written all over my face that I was still in the dark about the promotion.

'Haven't you spoken to Ian?' he asked.

I explained that Ian was travelling, but I had seen him two weeks prior, and he hadn't mentioned anything about a promotion.

'Sorry, I guess I've spoken out of turn, please don't say anything,' he said.

When Ian returned from his trip he came straight to the issue. 'I understand the cat is out of the bag,' he said in our first conversation.

'Yes, but I'm confused as to why I didn't hear about this from you,' I replied. 'It seems the committee approved the promotion last quarter.'

'That's true,' he acknowledged. 'I submitted your name last quarter before you had delivered on Project X – I was so confident that you would deliver, I didn't want to wait for the next cycle.'

For various reasons I had yet to complete the project he mentioned, but I had already achieved more than enough to merit the promotion, even without that delivery.

'I was waiting for you to deliver the project. I wanted the promotion to be a reward,' he said frankly, which was his way.

I was very upset. After all, if the committee felt I had earned my promotion, why should Ian block it? I felt it was wrong for him to withhold my promotion because of a single project that was in fact a cherry on top of my other accomplishments. I decided to call our HR director, Dave van Eeden.

'Can Ian actually do this?' I asked.

'Look, I knew your promotion had gone through, but I've been waiting for Ian to sign off,' he replied.

'But is there anything I can do about it?' I asked.

'I would sleep on it,' he advised. 'You know Ian is always your champion. Talk to him about why he hasn't put it through.'

The next day I met with Ian again, expressing my grievance.

'Nolitha, as your mentor and your champion in the organisation, you must know that I have your best interests at heart. I know you have delivered enough to deserve the promotion, but I'm pushing for you to deliver beyond what your peers are doing. The reality is that there are people here who have not fully accepted that you as the young, black woman in this organisation are achieving everything you have. They think that as your mentor, I am invested in making you look good. Because of that we have to take your project milestones and commitments very seriously. Not delivering on that project may not seem like a big deal to you, but it makes you and those supporting your cause look bad,' he explained.

It was a hard pill to swallow. Ultimately, however, I appreciated that as my mentor and boss, Ian did not spare me the tough messages. It may not have been fair that I needed to do more than others to prove myself, but it was true. And because I knew Ian was on my side, I could trust that his decision came from a good place, even if I did not agree with it.

The incident was a reminder of the importance of transparently addressing problems, and having honest and open discussions in a non-confrontational way to avoid misunderstandings. In particular, when you are in the middle of a professional argument, whether with your peers or boss – you feel you have been wronged and have reason to be outraged and upset – it does not help your case to push further with someone whom you know has always had your back.

Having reflected on that incident since, I have imagined what would have happened if I had gone above Ian and made a scene. Legally I would have been within my rights to do so, but I suspect that such an action would not have benefited the rest of my stay at Woolies. I had a trust relationship with Ian, so I did not need to escalate the issue and had I done so, it could have broken that trust. Though I never fully agreed with Ian's decision, I am glad I had the emotional maturity to discuss the problem, make my point and then move on. The policy of 'sleeping on it' paid off time and time again throughout my career. My relationship with Ian as my mentor and cheerleader went beyond my Woolies stay. Years later when I was nominated as the BMF president Ian was my escort for the gala dinner; beside my mother, I could not think of anyone better than him to do the honours.

Network exposure

In September 1997 while I was head of Corporate Affairs at Woolies, the BMF nominated me to participate in the first cohort of the Senior Executive Programme (SEP). Jointly run by Harvard University and the University of the Witwatersrand, the programme was intended to develop leadership capacity in our new democracy. Having received two USAID partial scholarships for 'civil society' participants, the BMF reviewed its national membership and ended up sending me and Mzwanele Manyi, who worked for Toyota SA. While the scholarship paid for 50% of our costs, our respective companies covered the balance – once again modelling the behaviour of companies that 'walk the talk' when it comes to developing staff for leadership.

The SEP accepted black professionals from both the public and private sectors, and there were about 60 of us from across the country, representing chief directors, senior managers and senior executives from across the spectrum. Like so many development programmes, many of our most valuable learnings came from interactions with other participants. Harvard used a case study methodology, and it was fascinating to see how each person approached the cases and devised solutions based on his or her different perspective or background.

The network exposure was incredible. Participating in that programme with 60 of the top up and coming black professionals from different sectors and industries, many of whom were already high flyers and key decision-makers, raised the bar in terms of how I viewed my own career and ambitions. Those peers became the examples I would later consider when mapping my own career progression, successes and challenges. Many of them became the people with whom, over the years, I spent time in intellectual conversation, as well as the people I knew I could call on moving forward.

◇◇◇◇

Soon after returning from the SEP, I took on my fourth and final role at Woolworths. As head of Corporate Affairs, my job had been about connecting the dots, pulling in different strategic strands, and considering all the angles, always asking what we were trying to achieve, what was the big picture, and how could we best position ourselves to achieve our goals. It was in that role that I truly came into my own as a strategist, having developed the sense of what I could comfortably do, and ceasing to second-guess myself unnecessarily.

In early 1998 I was promoted to be the head of HR in Retail Operations, my name having been put forward by another of my great Woolworths mentors, Simon Susman. This was the same man who eight years earlier had interceded on my behalf at the customer service counter in the days when I was a trainee in Wynberg and he was head of Retail Operations.

Now managing director, Simon and I had been having 'coffee conversations' since 1996. That relationship began thanks to a group session to which I had been invited as one of the 'high potential' young people in the company, back when I was still working in HR under Dave van Eeden. Eight of us, black and white, had been invited to a two-day 'blue sky' session with top leadership to discuss company strategy and the future. It was there that Simon took the time to speak to each of us, asking who we were, what our family background was like, how long we had been with the company, what we thought of the business, and what we felt the company should be doing or not doing. After that initial conversation he opened the door to all of us to drop in regularly, to come and speak and have a coffee, even if only once a year.

Simon and I had been having these 'coffee conversations' for a couple of years when the company decided to change the structure of its retail operations. With 110 stores and over 10 000 employees whose training, customer service and product knowledge needed to be up to standard, Retail Operations was the company's largest division and its heartbeat. Simon put my name forward for the job of head of HR of the Retail Division.

The company wanted to institute a huge turnaround programme for its retail systems, computerising and automating a new supply chain system to better understand and manage the movement of stock. Lacking any such comprehensive system until now (these were still the days of fax machines and only one computer per floor in our stores), information like how many units of a certain item were sold per day had to be calculated manually, which meant that if, for example, a customer wanted a product that a shop didn't have, there was no way to know if that item was unavailable only in that store or if it simply wasn't available. In fact, Woolworths used to stay open late on Wednesdays for the purpose of stock counting and trading.

Although the new retail system was a much needed upgrade in terms of tracking stock and numbers, its implementation obviously was worrying for staff. As with any systems process, a more simplified and efficient way of doing things meant fewer people were required to do them; with a scanning machine automatically updating the system with every purchase, the need to take stock on a weekly basis became unnecessary. The main challenge as HR head was getting staff buy-in for this new system.

'Change management' is never easy, but the workshops we ran to handle the transition served both as a training ground about how the new system worked and also as a platform where we could discuss the concerns and benefits to staff of the new system. In these workshops I came to deeply appreciate the astonishing amount of information that our people who dealt with customers every day had at their fingertips. Salespeople could tell you what was selling, why it was selling, and what the customers were saying. They also had important insights on why things weren't selling, often noting trends about what had sold the previous season in terms of colours, sizes and styles. All of this was a good reminder that nothing can replace good people.

◇◇◇◇◇

It was during my time as HR head in Retail Ops that I got my first taste of working closely with the unions, an eye-opening experience to say the least. Union members had previously known that when they engaged with management, this mainly meant dealing with white managers. This being the case, I went in thinking that because I was a black manager they would see me differently. Despite my familiarity with and sympathy for their issues, I quickly came to understand that to labour, I represented management and was therefore sometimes perceived as part of 'the problem'.

My engagement with unions further brought home the necessity of listening to each person's view and perspective and the extent to which the adversarial state of race relations had created a foundation of mistrust between management and staff. In those days I often travelled to Gauteng for monthly meetings held between management and labour union staff, where we discussed various topics from race issues in the stores to implementation problems around working processes.

I remember once arriving early for a meeting at our regional offices in Centurion, Pretoria. When I got there, about eight union members were already present. Beginning to chat with them, I went to make myself some tea, only to find there was no hot water in the thermos. When I asked the assistant for water she told me she hadn't brought it yet because the management team was still elsewhere. When she returned with the flask of hot water and I started pouring myself tea and offering tea to the guys, they started giggling.

'What's so funny?' I asked.

'Things have changed,' one of them said. 'Management is offering us tea!' He said it as if it was a joke.

'Come again?' I said, seeking clarity.

'You know we're not supposed to drink tea or touch the scones or biscuits before management comes,' the man said.

'What do you mean? You're here on time, waiting for others to arrive.'

'No, you don't understand the rules of this place. You can't have black people eating before white people,' the man retorted.

At this point my colleagues from management began to arrive and the conversation shifted. Later during the tea break I said to our host, who was my colleague, 'What's this I'm hearing from our union colleagues that they're not supposed to have tea before you guys come in? They are saying black people are not supposed to have tea before white people?'

'No, no, it's a long story,' he said. Then he explained that in the past the labour guys would come early to the meetings and eat all the food before anyone else arrived. Hence the institution of this general 'ban'.

With its patronising tones of mistrust, it sadly epitomised the relationship between labour and management. And because management was almost entirely white, and the unions were mainly black, the dynamic was further layered with whatever negative perceptions or interpretations people had of that (usually poor) racial relationship.

This shaky foundation meant that we started every engagement on a poor footing, and regardless of how simple or straightforward the issues on the meeting agenda might have been, they took longer to discuss because everyone was on eggshells.

Typically, meetings would begin with management stating a proposal. The union would then take five minutes to caucus and look into the issue, before coming back and asking things like: 'What do you mean by this word? What do you mean by that phrase? You said this in this way, what does that mean?' and so on. Management would then take five minutes to go and caucus its answers, then return and explain what was meant. This first part of the meeting was the process referred to as the 'questions for clarity'.

Next the unions would go back to caucus again, this time to ask the real questions or give a response on or counter-proposals to the actual proposal at hand: 'On this item this is what we think … On that item, this is how we feel.' Management would listen and go back out and caucus their own questions of clarity, returning to ask their substantive questions, and followed by the union caucusing to respond and come back with further questions of clarity.

This dance of caucusing and questions meant that an entire day could be consumed to cover just two agenda items. For each item, discussions that should have taken half an hour would take two hours, as we toiled simply to define terms and get on the same page, much less reach any agreement. It was incredibly frustrating. Watching the clock, you couldn't help but wonder where things were going, always aware that the whole meeting could degenerate into total dysfunction if we got stuck over a definition or something that someone thought they heard you say. Most of this stemmed from the deep and fundamental lack of trust between the two parties.

Over time, whenever we had to discuss contentious issues, I would arrive a day earlier, having already contacted representatives from the unions (whom I knew from my days of doing CSR) and requested an 'informal' conversation. These conversations often took place over coffee and sometimes after hours. In that less formal context, I could explain what we as management were trying to do, ask if it made sense and how they felt about it, and get a read on what the issues would be the next day so as to address and pre-empt them as much as possible.

These one-on-one meetings gave me the opportunity to really listen to people's perspectives and understand more deeply where they were coming from and why particular points mattered. I also heard directly from people whose specific perspectives were not always part of the formal meeting, where I only heard from the chairperson. In those informal meetings people were willing to offer personal suggestions or insights about how to do things, feedback I rarely heard in a formal session. Finally, these meetings were a 'safe space', where labour would sometimes share experiences of management from a cultural perspective, informing me if they thought a particular individual was not living the company's values or if a manager was consistently unfair.

Through these meetings I learned to listen: asking questions for clarity rather than jumping in to respond, and seeking first to understand. This meant probing with open-ended questions that allowed me to hear more and speak less: 'Why are you saying that? Why do you think it's like that?' I also learned to watch and read body language, as so often people express at least half of their message non-verbally.

I was not the only one having these informal sessions. Some of my colleagues in management did the same, but we all had our different relationships with the unions. There was no rulebook. It was up to you whether you wanted to suggest such a meeting, and up to the union if they would accept, as there were definitely people from management whom they would not meet. These meetings were about trust, and would happen only if they believed you would not abuse the knowledge you had gained through them.

When these sessions did occur, they usually made the official meeting that followed much more straightforward and efficient. That extremely frustrating process I described earlier could be simplified if not jettisoned. On both sides people were not so anxious or suspicious about why the other side was asking this question or that one, because the parties knew where they were going with it. Over time, engagements became more relaxed and you could see that we had built some trust between management and the unions.

I learned some invaluable lessons during my time as head of HR for Retail Ops. First was the importance of talking to people on the ground and appreciating the deep knowledge and unique perspectives they bring to the table. Woolworths was where I first understood that rather than sitting in your ivory tower thinking you have all the answers, you must go out and talk to the people on the shop floor: they will always tell you exactly what is happening, why it is happening the way it is, and what they believe can help turn a situation around. This lesson has served me well everywhere I have worked.

The second big learning for me, which came particularly through my engagement with the unions, was to understand that even though political transformation was changing the country, differences in economic empowerment between the haves and have nots remained largely unaffected. Once again it was clear to me that economic empowerment needed to be at the forefront of our transformation efforts, both as business leaders and as a nation.

National debates

The BMF's voice in the national debates around economic empowerment had continued to grow more confident, with BMF viewpoints championed by leading lights. In October 1997 the Western Cape Region successfully hosted the BMF's annual conference at the Spier wine estate in Stellenbosch.

PART 2: STEPPING OUT

Following Gavin's impressive drive to grow our membership, the Western Cape had become the largest BMF region by numbers: we had more members and programmes than the other regions, and thanks to Gavin and others, we were influencing the thinking in the country.

It was at the 1997 conference that the BMF came out with the resolution to set up a Black Economic Empowerment (BEE) commission, which became a gamechanger in terms of how BEE was perceived and taken up by government and the private sector. Cyril Ramaphosa, who was still a business leader at the time, was appointed chair of the commission, and Gavin Pietersen, who had been elected at the same conference as BMF national deputy president, was appointed as deputy chair of the committee. Following his appointment as deputy national president of the BMF, Gavin relinquished his regional chair role. I had served as Gavin's deputy since early 1996 and now I succeeded him as regional chair of the BMF for the Western Cape.

My responsibilities as regional chair were similar to those of being a branch chair but on a much bigger scale – engaging with more members and organising more dialogues, workshops and seminars. As the regional chair I had the additional role of serving on the BMF's national board, which was made up of all the regional chairs plus a few other members. Being part of the national board afforded me the platform to be involved in the national discussions that were taking place around the transformation laws and, in particular, BEE.

Before the BEE Act of 2003, there was the BEE Commission. Significantly informing the act, the commission was a direct outcome of the BMF's observation that although formal businesses had started 'doing empowerment', there was no well-understood framework or transparent process to engage with fundamental questions around how BEE was unfolding. In a completely ad hoc, self-driven fashion, companies would conduct a BEE transaction with so-and-so, selling a stake of 1% or 5%, and conclude that they had 'done their BEE'. But who said it should be 1% or 5%? And what criteria were used to choose the BEE partner? We needed a space to ask the right questions around what black economic empowerment meant and how it should be defined. How much should be given as part of the ownership discussion? And if ownership was being discussed, what was the appropriate quantum? And who determined what was appropriate?

The BEE Commission had been formed to grapple with such questions. This was another example of how the BMF picked up the issues of the time, engaged with them at a national level, pulled people in (many of whom were not necessarily formal fee-paying BMF members but were aligned with our agenda) and engaged with the right stakeholders, especially from government and labour, to lobby for our position.

◇◇◇◇◇

With my role as regional chair well entrenched, I played a new role – that of fundraiser. This meant selling the organisation's vision, programmes of action and reason for existence to corporates and other potential donors. In the post-1994 period, and with the new government in place and transformation laws being passed, members had begun questioning the need to keep the 'black' in the Black Management Forum. In other words, what was the BMF's relevance in the context of an ANC-led government supportive of transformation? Being forced to articulate the BMF's specific relevance to potential donors meant spending time with the branches interrogating exactly what the 'black' meant to us, and why it should be maintained instead of just 'Management Forum'.

In Cape Town, where distinctions between Coloureds and Africans continued to cause people to ask if a person was black or 'something else', this discussion was exceptionally vibrant. Under Gavin's leadership, the Western Cape BMF had taken great pride in being thought leaders around questions of African identity as well as change management training. Assisted by the CARAS Trust, with Margaret Wheatley as a master facilitator, Gavin had invested in anti-racism and anti-sexism training. Gavin was also brilliant at breaking down complex processes with great eloquence and passion, especially when it came to race and identity politics.

Because of all this awareness and education, to us at the BMF Western Cape, you were either Black or White: for us, 'Coloureds' or Indians who had suffered under apartheid were Black. If someone did not fundamentally identify as Black, we felt that person should not be part of the conversation examining why we should or should not keep the 'Black' in the BMF name, because their view was informed by a fundamentally different ideology.

For those of us who were on the same page, however, the next level of conversation examined the distinctions between black Africans as opposed to black coloureds or Indians, because after generations of being defined and constrained by these labels, it was important to acknowledge the historical and cultural differences they also pointed to. These ideological conversations around race – the question of the African identity and who was African – allowed us to recognise and unpack how racial definitions in South Africa were also still meaningful and in some cases appropriate. These debates often started at meetings and continued around braais, often over a few bottles of wine. Eventually, they built a sense of deep camaraderie and allowed for unusually high levels of honesty between our different racial groups.

These conversations were also happening against the backdrop of the enactment of the Employment Equity Act, which naturally included a large section defining Employment Equity beneficiaries, which were split by racial demographics. As such, we needed to defend and motivate for the necessity of those breakdowns; in other words, the act was not intended to separate people racially or use racial labelling for the sake of labelling, but did need to use demographic statistics to fix a historic problem built around such categories. Credibly selling these reasons for the BMF's existence with numerous and diverse stakeholders and potential donors led to many spirited boardroom discussions and expanded our Cape Town-based corporate membership.

My increasing involvement in the BMF leadership – first as Gavin's deputy, then Rondebosch branch chairperson, and finally Western Cape regional chairperson – greatly refined my leadership skills, which came to be defined by a consultative leadership style. In the Western Cape BMF I was surrounded by amazing peers – the likes of Zyda Rylands (current CEO of Woolworths SA), Barend Pieterse (chair, De Beers), Joe Mwase, Nadia Mason and Mphathi Nyewe – people who over the years have stayed the course in terms of leading change in industry in South Africa. Working with people of this calibre, all of whom were comrades from my peer group and leaders in their own right at their own companies, meant engaging in a way that respected each person's experience. It also carried the challenge of convincing these leaders who were as passionate about development and transformation as I was to trust me to lead them and the team.

In the end it was about earning people's trust that I would get the best out of each person. That came down to capturing and enhancing each person's unique contribution in terms of what they brought to the BMF, always trying to do so constructively and in a way that benefited the organisation and my leadership. Refining the team consultation approach that I had picked up while working with the unions, I focused on facilitating conversations to get the best out of individuals. That meant cultivating one-on-one discussions, listening, and always asking more questions.

Within the BMF at that time, we were very much aligned when it came to *what* to do, so most of our big debates and dialogues were about the *how*. People had very strong and often differing views, so that consultative leadership approach was key to building the trust needed to move forward on issues.

◇◇◇◇◇

At the end of 1997 – the year I was promoted to senior manager, participated in the SEP, and became BMF regional chair – I decided to send Phila to boarding school. Earlier that year Presto had started working in Joburg for Transnet and was commuting home to Cape Town fortnightly. With my life also so busy with travelling – as head of HR for Retail Ops, 80% of my business was outside the Western Cape – and with my increased BMF commitments, I knew something had to give. To be effective as a parent I needed to provide my son with consistency and stability, while to be effective at my job, I needed to know that I had my son covered.

Phila was ten years old when he started as a weekly boarder at Bishops Preparatory School in Cape Town. With Phila at boarding school I could be at work or involved in evening and weekend sessions with the BMF without worrying whether his homework was done or if he had been picked up. People sometimes asked if I felt guilty about this choice, but my perspective was that I was sending him to one of the country's top schools and had reflected on my own positive experiences in boarding school, which I had loved.

That said, it is not easy to raise a young child in a career like mine. On the days I wasn't travelling it was particularly tough, as I would want to fetch him from school, knowing that he was only 20 minutes away. But of course I knew that it wouldn't be productive to disrupt his routine. In the end it came down to self-awareness: knowing that I wanted to say yes to the opportunities that life was presenting, but also consciously making choices and organising my personal life in such a way that I could say yes and my child could thrive.

This decision links to a question I've often been asked around the country on how you know when you're ready for the next big challenge. Again, it goes back to self-awareness: being able to honestly and sincerely appraise your own strengths and weaknesses, and thus to know if you are mentally and emotionally ready. The emotional part is key, because a large part of readiness is understanding what moving to that next position you aspire to will take in terms of the commitment and sacrifices that come with the role.

In the case of my family situation, by this time I was running myself to a standstill between driving my son to school, being late for his afternoon pick-ups because I was stuck in meetings, rushing through homework and bedtime reading, I knew I was heading for a meltdown. Even though I had tried to put all the support structures in place for my child – such as convincing my mother to relocate from the Eastern Cape, and hiring an au pair – they had proved insufficient. So, boarding school became our best and most practical solution.

While it may not be acceptable for some people, it was a choice I made. By making that choice, I knew I was ready for other things. Although mental or intellectual readiness are obviously fundamental, it is the emotional readiness – where you've looked at all the upsides and downsides of what it would mean to go for that role and you've organised your life so that you can take them on – that allows people to go for the next big challenge.

By the year 2000 I was ready for a new challenge. Having served as BMF regional chairperson for two years, I was also in my second year as head of HR for Retail Ops at Woolworths when I received my ten-year certificate of service from the company. Soon thereafter I met Simon for one of our coffee conversations and told him I felt I needed a sabbatical.

The BMF would be celebrating its 25th anniversary the following year, and the organisation wanted to use that occasion to reposition itself. As our democracy had evolved through the late 90s, we as an organisation had affirmed the relevance of the 'B' in the BMF. As that conversation was settled, we also saw the need to refocus on how to best continue serving our agenda of developing managerial leadership and ensuring the inclusion of black people in the management and leadership of South African organisations and business.

At the time I did not want to leave Woolworths – a company whose values I truly believed in and a place where I had experienced so much growth – but I did want very much to participate fully in that dialogue to maintain the BMF's relevance. As always, Simon was supportive. In fact he was pleased that I wanted to use the sabbatical in this way, which is how I ended up being seconded by Woolworths to the BMF on my full salary for a year. My transition from Cape Town to Johannesburg had begun.

PART 3

◇◇◇◇◇◇◇◇◇◇◇◇◇

A NATIONAL STAGE

It doesn't interest me
Who you know or how you came to be here. I want to know if you
will stand in the center of the fire with me and not shrink back.
It doesn't interest me where or what or with whom you studied.
I want to know what sustains you, from the inside, when all else falls away.
I want to know if you can be alone with yourself and if you truly like
the company you keep in the empty moments.

ORIAH MOUNTAIN DREAMER

From *The Invitation*

CHAPTER 7

Synergistic symphonies: The power of collaborations

In early 2000 I began my secondment from Woolworths as a full-time employee at the BMF's head office in Sandton, Johannesburg. At Simon's suggestion, we made a point of meeting at least once a quarter, as much to keep me in touch with what was happening in the business as to ensure senior management didn't forget about me. This was wise, as I quickly got swept up in the enthusiasm that infused the BMF's head office during this period when our country was figuring out how to execute its new transformation laws.[4]

'I haven't seen you this excited in a long time. You are so passionate when you speak about the BMF,' Simon observed at our second meeting. He went on to say that it sounded like the things I wanted to achieve at the BMF would take longer than the year's secondment that Woolworths could support, and he gave me his blessing to move on.

Woolworths had been a wonderful company to be a part of. First, it gave me a career in which I had never been stagnant. Tasked with four different jobs over ten years, I had gained exposure to numerous areas of the business as well as leadership styles and cultures and sub-cultures within those various departments and divisions.

Second, it was at Woolworths that I had been provided a template for what it meant to be in a values-based organisation. Those values set the tone for the whole organisation and were fundamental to recruitment and promotion choices. Across all my positions from graduate trainee to senior manager, the importance of clear values-driven behaviour by the organisation's leaders was repeatedly demonstrated.

Finally, I had truly great mentors. Although I counted myself 'lucky' to have come across those particular individuals in my career, I believe that it was the company's adherence to its particular value system that drew this calibre of people (who, not unusual given the time, but notably, had mainly been white males). The point is that the quality of mentorship I received spoke to Woolworths' ability to attract high-quality people, which was the direct result of conscious management decisions rather than a stroke of good luck.

Among other things, my departure from Woolworths meant I could finally move to Joburg permanently. As much as I had been a regular business traveller to Joburg over the previous years, there is a huge difference between travelling to a place for work and calling it home. The fact that this city was now my home filled me with exhilaration. In a way this was odd, because had anyone asked, I would never have said I was unhappy in Cape Town. On the contrary, I could have stayed for years, feeling that I had everything I needed – family, friends, and even my mother.

By contrast, many of my black friends and associates experienced Cape Town as a deeply inhospitable place. My experiences of the Mother City differed not because I did not see or experience this exclusion, but rather because my fulfilling career progression, my son's happiness at his school, and the social camaraderie and intellectual stimulation that came from my close involvement with the Western Cape's incredibly diverse and close-knit BMF branches buffered me from the worst of it. That supportive environment also helped the eternal optimist in me continue to believe that Cape Town's negative racial dynamics were changing. I would often remind friends that we were only five years into liberation, and eventually the 'shock' would wear off and white Capetonians would accept the new reality.

In the meantime, my departure from the Western Cape brought with it an unanticipated sense of relief. Whether going to the movies, shopping at the mall or eating out at restaurants, I suddenly found myself back in a black majority in Joburg. Only then did I fully grasp how much being the only black person in so many given situations had been a burden. Oddly, the one space where I noted a disconnect in terms of the evolution of racial dynamics was at the BMF. As much as I enjoyed being in the black majority in Gauteng, our BMF meetings felt very homogenous compared with what I had grown used to in Cape Town, where 30% of our members were white, about 50% coloured, and the rest black Africans. As I have mentioned, that diversity and the challenging but ultimately positive conversations it engendered around what it meant to be 'black' in South Africa were a unique way in which the Western Cape BMF had been very advanced in terms of the nuance with which it handled racial dynamics. Under Ryland Fisher's editorship, the *Cape Times* ran a month-long series on race and diversity in Cape Town, a result of our many debates at the BMF. That said, relocating to Joburg was a homecoming for me: the release of a long breath I hadn't even realised I had been holding for all those years.

Managing director

Not long after I arrived at the BMF as a seconded employee, it became clear that health reasons would require the BMF's managing director, Neville Maimane, to withdraw early from his term, and he would be departing by year's end. When my colleagues at the BMF learned that I was open to leaving Woolworths permanently, someone suggested I apply for the managing director post, which is how by the end of 2000 I took the reins as the MD of the BMF.

My vision for my tenure as MD was twofold: one, to strengthen our operations and build a more effective membership-oriented organisation, and two, to support BMF president Bheki Sibiya's agenda to reaffirm our organisation's relevance by aligning our continued development of black managerial leadership with the implementation of the transformation laws that were unfolding.

From an operational perspective, I focused on financing and reinforcing our institutional frameworks at the national level. When I started as MD, I saw that although the BMF was meant to be a national organisation, our active branches were limited to four of our nine provinces (namely, Gauteng, KZN, the Western Cape and North West), in part due to budget deficits. Corporate fundraising, therefore, became my first priority. By the time I finished my term as MD in 2003, the BMF had extracted itself from its financial troubles and was operating with a sustainable annual operating revenue. As a mission-driven organisation, the BMF at the time relied heavily on fundraising to sustain its operations.

Meanwhile, my experience and familiarity with chainstore operations at Woolworths proved extremely valuable in taking our 'brand' to the next level. I understood both the replicating processes and standardisation of systems as well as the power of image and the need to project a coherent national identity as an organisation. To this end, we re-evaluated our systems and processes from the national level, aligning things from our branch constitutions to induction manuals and policies, as well as standardising basic admin – in some cases strengthening and in others creating these things where they did not previously exist.

In the interest of consolidating and amplifying our messaging, we also created various communications platforms. Firstly, to commemorate our 25th anniversary we published a coffee table book titled *Against All Odds*, which mapped the BMF's history over its 25 years of existence since 1976, something which had not been captured in one place prior to this publication. Secondly, we founded our own magazine, *African Leader*, both to promote our national image and brand, as well as to influence the conversation in the country around black leadership economic empowerment and corporate transformation. We found a publisher, created an editorial committee headed by Ms Wendy Luhabe as editor-in-chief, and ensured that our quarterly magazine was distributed and sold in Exclusive Books, South Africa's largest bookstore chain. Lastly, we created a website. The world wide web had recently come into South Africa's mainstream, and we realised the need to create and maintain a digital presence.

Finally, in the interest of increasing our value proposition to our members

My grandmother, Mangangenkomo (seated), with a friend.

My parents' wedding picture: Mr Victor Mthunzi Njoli and Miss Yolisa Nodumo Ntuthu (1963).

Me, aged four.

At the Miss Freshette competition at the University of Fort Hare (1982).

The Fakude bridal party at my home in Cenyu Village, Stutterheim. I am seated on the floor with my mother, Dumo (1989).

The Njoli bridal party in Stutterheim (1989).

Celebrating graduation day – a BA Honours from the University of Fort Hare – with my mother, Dumo (1990).

The BMF Western Cape board members with Dr Naledi Pandor (centre) at the BMF Western Cape Awards (1997).

At the 1997 BMF Western Cape Awards with (from left) Gavin Pieterse (president), me (deputy president), Dr Naledi Pandor (MP) and Ryland Fischer (editor of the *Cape Times*).

With our friend Cynthia Mkhize and Winnie Madikizela-Mandela while Mama Winnie was staying with us in Cape Town (1994).

BMF national board members with Bheki Sibiya as president (right of front row) and Bonang Mohale as deputy president (centre of front row) (1999).

At the BMF annual conference with fellow board member and friend Ms Mandiza Mbekeni and a conference attendee (2002).

Giving the managing director's report at the BMF annual general meeting (2002).

With Bheki Sibiya at the BMF national conference (2002).

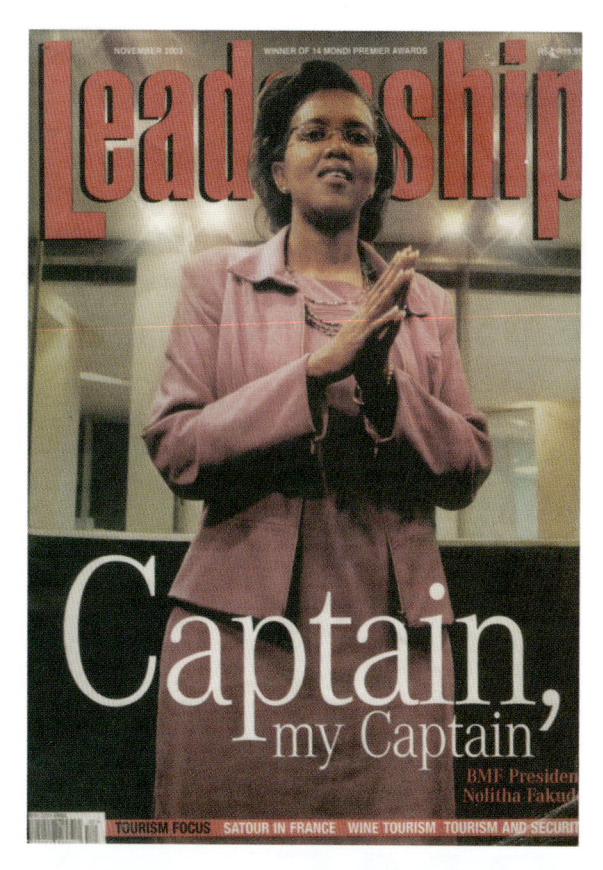

On the cover of *Leadership* magazine (2003).

President Thabo Mbeki with BMF board members at the national conference (2003).

With BMF national board members at the World Economic Forum in Davos (2004).

Thanksgiving at home celebrating my Sasol appointment (2005).

The *African Leader* magazine, BMF's official publication, was launched in 2000. With me on this 2007 cover are Mzwanele Manyi (president), Lot Ndlovu (former BMF president) and Wendy Luhabe (BMF stalwart).

Family portrait, with my siblings, Siyolo, Vuyelwa and Vuyo, and with my mother, Dumo, and son, Phila, at his 21st birthday celebration (2010).

Phila's graduation at the University of the Witwatersrand, with my mother, Dumo (2012).

The Human Resource Development Council, chaired by then Deputy President Kgalema Motlanthe (2013).

Sasol EXCO members at the New York Stock Exchange, celebrating ten years of Sasol listing.
IMAGE COURTESY OF SASOL

With Sasol chairman, Hixonia Nyasulu, after the annual general meeting (2013).

With Sasol's executive directors in New York, Christine Ramon and David Constable.
IMAGE COURTESY OF SASOL

At a sports awards dinner, hosted by the national minister of sport, with an award in recognition for the role I played in promoting women's sports, specifically Banyana Banyana (2015).

With my family and friends at the Sasol Annual Chairman's Dinner. From left to right: David Constable, Max Sisulu, Phila Fakude, Colin Hall, Dumo Njoli, Mandiza Mbekeni, Brenda Constable, George Suliali and Elinor Sisulu (2016).

Sasol farewell dinner with Sasol board members, Nomgando Matyumza and Imogen Mkhize, and former Sasol chairman, Hixonia Nyasulu (2016).

Banners showing some of the former BMF presidents at the BMF's 40th anniversary in 2016: Lot Ndlovu (1995–1999), Bheki Sibiya (1999–2003), Nolitha Fakude (2003–2006) and Mzwanele Manyi (2006–2012).

Attending Mama Winnie Madikizela-Mandela's funeral with my son, Phila (2018).

What's left of NoDumo Cash Store in 2019. A customer with my brother, Vuyo (in the black coat).

as well as catalysing them to act as change agents in their own workplaces, we increased seminars and training opportunities. Topics ranged from general leadership to corporate governance and corporate activism, the last mentioned being something for which the BMF was known historically. Looking to the next generation, we appointed young graduates onto learnerships and internships in the BMF. This had the dual purpose of grooming a new cadre of young people while also expanding capacity in our branches and head office, which, when I arrived in 2000 had only four full-time staff, a number that tripled to twelve by the end of my term in 2003. With one of the big audit firms (Deloitte), we ran corporate governance workshops focusing on new directors, as we wanted to increase the pipeline and pool of black directors.

Sector charters

In addition to growing the BMF from an operational perspective, I supported the board's mission to realign its priorities and reorient its vision. With the enactment of the transformation laws taking centre stage, we focused our energies on the key areas of sector charters, skills development and employment equity. The BEE Act of 2003 would soon define and guide the country's larger transformation strategy and principles, but in the meantime we had to buckle down and figure out how to make these things work practically. This was where the sector charters, which focused on execution and delivery, came in.

Since 1997, most of the country's largest sectors – financial services, mining, liquid fuels, ICT, and property/construction – had at least started to design the sector charters that would guide the implementation of their respective sectors' transformation commitment. Broadly speaking, this meant outlining processes to implement the charter, setting practical targets and timelines, and creating mechanisms to monitor and report on progress (for example, tools like scorecards, investment guidelines, and guidelines on engaging with other stakeholders).

The sector charters were co-created in government-led consultation forums where the private sector and black business associations had an equal voice. The equal inclusion of black business associations in the charter drafting process came about thanks to the BEE Commission, where concerns had been raised around adequate black representation in the 'private sector' stakeholder category, which at the time skewed heavily white. As such, relevant black business associations from each industry participated in the discussions around targets, processes to implement the charters and mechanisms to monitor and report on progress. ABSIP (the Association of Black Securities and Investment Professionals) led financial services; the Junior Miners in the Chamber led the mining charter; AMEF led Liquid Fuels; ICT was led by the BITF (Black Information Technology Forum); and property and construction was led by the department of Public Enterprises. Discussions pertaining to all sectors incorporated inputs from sister organisations. It was in this capacity, as a 'sister organisation', that the BMF – a major black business association with a significant, broad and diverse membership base that it could access and mobilise to engage in the necessary discussions – took part.

The BMF's most direct contribution to the charter drafting process was our work around target-setting for employment equity and skills development. To this end, we established a Policy Research desk, sponsored by Metropolitan (one of our corporate members). Headed by Mxolisi Lindi, whom we recruited from the National Treasury, this unit collected and compiled the research, benchmarks and statistics required to set realistic targets. Where information did not exist – for example, data reflecting the experiences of people on the ground concerning things such as difficulties around accessing finance as a black businessperson – the unit worked with our branches and members to compile figures.

This was one of the busiest periods in my career, a time filled with great wisdom largely gained from fellow black business leaders and key stakeholders. Gwede Mantashe was one of these stakeholders, and I still remember my first conversation with this great and pragmatic strategist.

I had been MD for about six months when I received a call from Mr Mantashe, a man I had never met but knew was the Secretary General of the National Union of Mineworkers (NUM), the powerful trade union which, with over 300 000 members, was and is the largest affiliate of COSATU.[5] I quickly learned he was also very direct.

'Ms Fakude, I'm told that you are the new boss of the BMF,' said the voice on the other end of the line.

I replied that the boss of the BMF was our president, Bheki Sibiya – who was also my boss.

'No,' he interrupted, 'Lot Ndlovu told me that you are the "man in charge" at the BMF these days,' he said.

Mantashe went on to explain that the reason he was calling was that he wanted NUM and the BMF to collaborate on driving the employment equity and skills development issues within the private sector. 'Working together will be key to the success of these transformation charters that everyone is busy with,' he said.

'Yes, sir, I fully agree,' I responded, then added, 'However, I'm not sure exactly whom I should be speaking with.'

Mantashe spent the next half hour educating me about how best the BMF could play its role across the various sectors and with other professional and business associations as well as with all the unions. He emphasised the importance of ensuring that all the charters had a common and consistent approach to setting targets for representation (that is, employment equity) as well as developing and building the capacity of black professionals to be ready for senior-level opportunities as they arose.

Compromise and negotiation

My involvement in the sector charters really brought home the extent to which the skills development issue was (and still is) so fundamental to the successful achievement of employment equity. In response to setting diversity targets, you constantly hear people saying, 'But we don't have the skills in our sector. We don't know where to find the women or black people who are suitably qualified.' Which is exactly where the vital discussion about skills and training investments comes in, and where the charters helped us to define and lay out a strategy for skills development in each sector.

In short, the private sector needed to spend money to set up time for skills development and training, as well as to create bursaries to develop the necessary pipeline of skills and people to come through the ranks in each sector so that charter targets could be met over time. Given the history of our country, all stakeholders shared a common understanding around the lack of development opportunities for black people, but acknowledging this need and agreeing on and committing to the skills development programmes to help address it were very different things.

Although both the employment equity and skills development targets are discretionary, meeting skills development targets requires companies to dedicate the resources to train people. Because of this, skills development training is both the first place short-sighted companies look when cutting budgets, as well as an area often neglected by small companies, which figure someone bigger will take it on. As with any collective effort, this incremental 'ducking' adds up, contributing to our inability as a country to hit our employment equity targets and to fill the talent pipeline with the skills that we need. A consequence on a more localised level is that when opportunities do arise, those companies that have not provided adequate internal training will not have people ready to take up positions, leading to poaching from companies that have been training. Larger companies are thus put in the frustrating position of training for the industry, which on one level they accept, but is also discouraging. This troublesome practice remains true and problematic to this day.

SYNERGISTIC SYMPHONIES: COLLABORATIONS

⋄⋄⋄⋄⋄

As MD of the BMF, I worked most closely in the HR workstream of the financial sector charter group, but also participated in most of the charter discussions, mainly aiming to ensure continuity and consistency in our approach to these processes and negotiations across sectors.

Despite all the good faith collaboration and open consultation that marked these discussions, negotiating targets amid the often competing priorities of government, business and labour was extremely complex. Each sector needed to agree on a target for employment equity and ownership, as well as the investment amount for skills development, depending on the sector. The targets were all very specific to the industry in terms of what and how much they should be doing by when. For example, the financial services sector charter set a target of 10% black ownership by 2014, while the mining charter said 26% by 2014. Meanwhile 1% of the wage salary bill was to be spent on skills development across all sectors, via the skills levy that every company pays by law.[6] The charters also set targets for things such as how much businesses in that sector should be spending on social responsibility in the areas where they operated. Progress towards agreed-to targets would be monitored using 'BEE scorecards', and minimum scores would be required to be considered for business opportunities such as desirable government tenders.

Negotiating targets and discussing what kind of interventions needed to be put in place to ensure that those targets were achievable with all the relevant stakeholders was a predictably lengthy process. For example, having left a workshop where you had finally reached agreement on the broader range for a particular target, a week later you would read that a much narrower number that had not even been on the table had just been approved as law. Such was the nature of the target setting in the early 2000s.

Frustrating as this was at the time, we had to let some of these things go. While we agreed that a consultative target-setting process was necessary, we also knew it needed to conclude swiftly. Our transformation journey, which had begun with the creation of the BEE Commission in 1997, was now reaching an important milestone in the finalising of our country's sector charters. The urgent need to move to implementation meant we could not afford to quibble endlessly over a few percentage points here or there. Twenty years later some of us feel very differently about this good faith consultative process. Particularly in light of the lack of progress made by different business sectors, we have been forced to question the decision to let businesses set their own targets, especially around employment equity and skills development.

At the time, however, it felt like a marvel that the first five sector charters – mining, liquid fuel, financial, ICT, and property/construction – were signed and adopted within ten years of founding our democracy. Although many people believed we should have completed them sooner, even now, a quarter century into our democracy, debates continue to rage about BEE targets in each sector.

A case in point is the BMF's call since 2004 for an 'economic CODESA'. The original 1991 CODESA, or the Convention for a Democratic South Africa, united 92 organisations bonded by their opposition to apartheid, and succeeded in clarifying a blueprint and mechanisms for the transition of political leadership, including a non-partisan transition government. At this point in our democracy, looking at the economic disempowerment that still so disproportionately plagues black people and women, we must find a way to get past the political controversies and private sector disagreements that hamper the achievement of economic justice.

Culture change

The third main area of BMF focus from 2001 to 2003 was leadership and culture change. The BMF's core philosophy advocated for organisations to change their culture to enable black people and women to grow and prosper in their organisations, rather than expecting these individuals to assimilate to an existing culture. To get a clearer sense of what was happening on the ground, we engaged with private sector leaders to examine company programmes directly, and also asked our own members to survey and assess the workshops held around diversity and inclusion in the companies where they worked.

What soon became apparent about corporate culture on the whole was that as a black person or woman, more often than not, you were expected to change and adapt to an organisation's existing culture. Our view was that organisations needed to create new identities and cultures that accommodated the people who were now coming into them. The culture question was not just about people feeling welcomed or comfortable, but went straight to the issue of who gets promoted within an organisation, who is put through development programmes, and who is appointed to key decision-making positions. Black or white, male or female, the people you promote, support and develop sends a message to the organisation about the face of success: that is, who does the organisation elevate to be seen as a role model? Those choices are often informed and influenced by a company's culture. Too many black employees continued to feel alienated, unappreciated and invisible within their working environments. Our survey results thus confirmed the need across our members' companies to run more culture change and diversity and inclusion programmes.

I personally met with most of the BMF corporate member companies, on the one hand presenting our survey results, and on the other offering the BMF's support in terms of connecting them to our members, as well as to tried and trusted companies in the field of diversity – for example, Stanley Mbongwe's Diversity Institute, Nene Molefi's Mandate Molefi, and so many other companies owned and run by black people – that could help them execute the culture change work required.

Generally speaking, the BMF did not have any direct accounts (that is, it did not run culture change programmes itself). It served rather as a facilitator to make introductions, raise awareness and occasionally run a culture change and transformation session when a company invited us to address its board of directors. In those latter cases, we would speak about the BMF's vision and mission, the issues we felt were key around diversity and transformation, and ways companies could work with the BMF and other black business associations to further their culture change agendas, particularly focusing on leadership. These meetings with corporate member boards fed directly into my fundraising role, in that they presented opportunities to demonstrate the BMF's value add, and how their association with us could benefit their culture change initiatives. Although we got great uptake, culture change remains an ongoing challenge and process – this is not an area where you can host one session and think you are done.

At the time, our focus on questions of culture highlighted for me the challenges we still faced around the visibility (or lack thereof) of women leaders in the private sector. Even at the BMF, it became increasingly clear that we had probably spent too long focusing on race to the exclusion of gender. Because of this we lacked a synchronised approach to race and gender transformation that consistently dealt with them in the same way. Then and now, particularly in the private sector, there are still so few women sitting in key decision-making positions. It was high time to challenge that status quo and find ways for more women to access leadership opportunities.

One business voice

As previously indicated, the BMF has a number of sister organisations with which we continued to collaborate on many nation-building projects. One of these came early on in my BMF presidency. The business associations were given a task and a challenge by the then South African President Thabo Mbeki. His question and his message were clear: 'Why is it that we still don't have one voice of business in South Africa?' and 'Sort yourselves out!'

This resulted in all business formations, both the previously white and black ones, getting together to structure this new path. The black organisations came under the umbrella of the then Black Business Council (BBC), and the white under Business South Africa (BSA). The BMF was represented at various levels within the BBC by myself, Bheki Sibiya and Lot Ndlovu. Lot was a member of the council; Bheki and myself served on its different workstreams.

SYNERGISTIC SYMPHONIES: COLLABORATIONS

I remember some of the members of our workstream – two of whom were Advocate Dali Mpofu (BITF) and David Moshapalo (FABCOS) – which was looking at drafting the proposed terms of reference, furiously working towards a deadline that required us to circulate these to the other BBC members, like NAFCOC, NBBC, ABASA and others. Once these were agreed upon, they were forwarded to the BSA team for discussion. So much was happening during that process but what stands out for me was the intense lobbying within the BBC membership to put forward names for office bearers, particularly for the top two positions of the soon-to-be-formed business organisation.

One name that kept coming up consistently was Patrice Motsepe, coming from NAFCOC. At the time Patrice was very reluctant to accept this nomination as his businesses were still in their early stages of growth and he felt that he needed more time to focus entirely on them. After much persuasion, he relented and agreed to come on board provided the new organisation would have a strong CEO and support structure to get things going and execute the new strategy. The BMF was asked to nominate a candidate for the CEO position and after careful consideration, we nominated Bheki Sibiya for the role. At the time Bheki was one of the executive directors of Transnet as well as one of the strongest general managers in the country. The BSA put forward an equally strong nomination in Bobby Godsell for the top position. Bobby was at the time CEO of AngloGold Ashanti. As a result, and in a unified compromise, we ended up with the top leadership team of Business Unity South Africa (BUSA), the voice of business having equal representation from the BSA and BBC. Also in 2003 Patrice was named president of BUSA and Bobby chairman in the presence of President Mbeki at an event held in Sun City.

Both organisations had made a commitment to give BUSA their full support and co-operation in order to make it a success. The department of Trade and Industry was tasked by President Mbeki to support BUSA during the first few years of its existence.

However, I was puzzled when a few months after the launch of BUSA,

I came across a letter from a newly formed organisation called Business Leadership South Africa (BLSA).

One of the stated objectives at the time for setting up BLSA was to ensure co-ordination of the top listed companies in order for them to allegedly enhance their participation at BUSA. Consequently, the BBC disbanded once BUSA was formed, with the understanding that at some point another co-ordinating body would be formed in its place. Unfortunately, this was not to be for the following seven years and the black business associations lost their momentum in terms of their participation within BUSA. I believe this unintended hiatus may have contributed a lot in the ensuing debates within and among black business associations about the real mandate of BUSA. The concern expressed was whether it really articulated the issues and challenges faced by black business people and professionals in making a breakthrough with the economic transformation agenda of South African businesses.

In the past five years, the BBC has become much stronger and more confident as they strive to rediscover and reassert their voice and carve their space on the broader economic growth and transformation agenda.

Personally, I believe that BUSA owes it to all of us to facilitate a much more cohesive and constructive way forward towards all of its members and to finding one another, otherwise it is counter-productive to talk about business unity in the absence of the spirit for which it was originally intended.

CHAPTER 8

◇◇◇◇◇◇◇◇◇◇◇◇◇◇◇◇

(Redefining) a woman's place

It was early 2003, the last year of my term as MD, when BMF president Bheki Sibiya announced that he would not stand for a second term, provided the BMF elected a woman as its next president. A leader in both the public and private sectors, Bheki was a true believer in the principles of fairness, equality and justice, and his thinking was consistently ahead of the curve. Another one of my great mentors who raised me in the BMF, Bheki remains one of my 'go to' people when I am grappling with an issue and need a different perspective or sounding board.

Bheki would have easily won a second term as BMF president had he run, but he believed it was time for a woman to step in. By the early 2000s, the private sector culture change focus in terms of race was remarkable, but the visibility and voices of female leaders remained negligible. Although realising gender equality in business leadership was by no means the responsibility of black transformation leaders alone, we were the ones driving the broader transformation agenda and we had allowed gender to take a back seat.

I believe that black people's long exclusion under apartheid caused some men to harbour a view that black females were crowding 'their' space when things finally started opening up in 1994. In other words, the patriarchy wanted us to wait at the back of the queue. I clearly recall a discussion on gender at the 1995 BMF conference at Joburg's Carlton Centre, in which a male delegate admonished us women to 'wait our turn', perhaps echoing a sentiment held by many at the time. Although a robust debate ensued, with the likes of Ms Naledi Pandor, Advocate Cawe Mahlathi and Ms Nyami Mandindi pushing back forcefully, it seemed, at least in the private sector, that we had somehow acquiesced.

It was in this context that Bheki's decision was so significant: its symbolism reflecting the seriousness of the BMF's intent to put the gender agenda back on the table. For any change process to move forward effectively, there are certain initial steps that leaders have got to take, and more often than not these are symbolic actions that show commitment to the particular agenda for change. For a business, seemingly small things such as abolishing reserved parking or executive dining rooms are symbolic acts that may not necessarily change the bottom line, but send powerful messages from leadership to say we are serious about change and things are going to be done differently. I strongly believe in the importance of symbolic actions from top leadership to support effective culture change initiatives, and Bheki's choice to step down on the condition that the BMF looked for a female candidate was a message that came through loud and clear.

Although Bheki was already reaching out to the national BMF leadership to test their readiness for this shift and to identify prospective female candidates, he also asked me as MD to supply him with some names. This was not difficult, as we already had a very capable and competent pool of female leaders such as deputy president Cecilia Khuzwayo (who was also chair of the SABC board), as well as several other suitable and senior BMF women.

However, returning from his conversations with national leadership a few weeks later, Bheki informed me that mine was the name that was coming up most frequently. Would I consider running? he asked. I was surprised and honoured by the suggestion, but also very aware of unspoken protocols around leadership progression, and I did not want to jump in to claim the title. I went to Cecilia, who said she had indeed considered the role but felt that my youth, energy and full-time engagement as an executive the last few years made me the best candidate. In terms of my own aspirations, I had seen many of my peers and predecessors pass through what appeared a natural progression from branch chair to regional chair to the pinnacle of president. It was a role to which I certainly aspired, but I had expected a second term as MD, and only seen the presidency as a goal for perhaps five years hence.

With requests from over half of the BMF regional chairs to forward my name as someone who could lead the organisation with credibility and integrity, I decided I needed to have a frank chat with some of my male colleagues. There were several individuals who could have easily contested my nomination and become president themselves, and I knew that by stepping back in order to support this step forward for the organisation, they were sacrificing something. As such, I wanted to be sure I knew where certain people stood when it came to my nomination and potential presidency, as half-hearted support from key people would have minimised my effectiveness. Consulting with a colleague such as Bonang Mohale (who ended up passionately lobbying for my nomination with other branches) allowed me to whole-heartedly embrace, own and thus contribute fully to my next leadership role.

A breakthrough for the gender agenda

By the time we went to our annual general meeting in October 2003, I was running unopposed for BMF president. In a career blessed by opportunities and filled with humbling moments, becoming BMF president was among the most humbling. The significance of it all – that moment when you look at the bigger scheme of things and ask yourself, 'But how did I get here?' – began to creep into my consciousness the morning after my election, when we received a message that President Thabo Mbeki intended to come congratulate us on this step that the organisation had taken in appointing a female president. President Mbeki's words on the last day of our conference in Cape Town were a great affirmation, but the full reality still was to hit days and even weeks later.

The morning after my election, I flew home to Joburg, unaware that news of my presidency at the BMF had been on the front page of *Business Day* and pretty much every other national newspaper. In fact, the media had loved a particular part of my speech, which had made it into several articles. Responding to the inevitable questions around how I was going to fill Lot's (Ndlovu) and Bheki's (Sibiya) shoes, I had made it clear that I did not intend to wear men's shoes. Rather, woman that I am, I was bringing five pairs of shoes into my presidency. They included high heels (to stand tall and look my male peers straight in the eye); sneakers (so I could be agile, running and skipping as necessary to navigate this leadership role); sandals with flowers (so I don't take myself too seriously); boots with spikes (to kick butt); and slippers (for tiptoeing and moving stealthily). Finally, I also said that sometimes I would walk barefoot, to stay humble and keep in touch with mother nature and my ancestors.

Arriving to an empty home that Saturday morning, as I opened the front door, I felt a resistance on the other side. Pushing harder, I found the entrance of my house transformed into what looked like a florist. I still don't know how my staff managed to close the door. In retrospect I figured they must have exited through the garage. In any case, my first thought when seeing all those flowers was concern that something bad had happened.

One of the first cards I opened was from then first lady Mrs Zanele Mbeki. The next few bunches were congratulations from the majority of our female cabinet ministers. On it went, with about a dozen bouquets and baskets from the CEOs and MDs of various companies – Absa's Nallie Bosman, FirstRand's Paul Harris, and Nando's Kevin Utian (who made hilarious reference to my speech, proclaiming Nando's confidence that I would 'fill "all five pairs of shoes", walk "barefoot" peri-proudly, and fly high') – some of whom I personally didn't even know at that stage. Finally there were the dozens of messages of goodwill from a wide range of stakeholders on cards and letters, many of which I still have today.

Taking it all in, I had a complete meltdown. I literally sat on the floor and wept as it hit me for the first time that through me, the BMF had sent a deliberate symbolic message to the rest of the country to say gender equality matters, it is important to the business agenda, and we needed to and would do more to step up our game. Staring at all those flowers and cards, I was overwhelmed by the extent to which that message was being embraced, and how much goodwill and support there was for it. I also realised the extent to which people were counting on me to fulfil that promise.

I saw with great clarity that being appointed like this had little to do with me being 'the one' but rather everything to do with the organisation's requirements for a leader at that particular point and time. As I have mentioned, other colleagues like Cecilia and Bonang would have been perfectly suitable to run the organisation, but in terms of the life cycle of the BMF and where it was at, I was probably the most appropriate. I was reminded of what Ian Sturrock used to say about being 'first among equals'. Placed in a leadership position like that, you quickly become aware that although you are sitting there now, there are ten others who are ready and possibly even better than you, but you have been given this opportunity because for various reasons – some of which may have little to do with your distinguished personal achievements – you are the best match at that time.

With that understanding comes both humility and pressure to deliver, as you realise that you are not the leader because you are 'the best' or the smartest. Rather you are there representing other people's aspirations. For me this translated into a renewed commitment to consulting with people, engaging with all my stakeholders, and taking on board viewpoints that under normal circumstances I would not even have considered before making business decisions. Fortunately, it turned out that such a consultative approach has tremendous benefits for change management.

During the period that followed I also became highly aware of the need to be fully centred as a person. Although I had so much support from colleagues, peers and stakeholders, it was vital that I understood myself, as self-awareness is core to finding one's centre as an individual. Self-awareness comes from the ability to reflect, be still and to listen to your inner voice. Such groundedness is also what allows you to listen for the quieter voices in a room, especially when in the midst of busy or heated discussions. If you are not able to be still, reflective and centred, you will miss out on the voices that may not be shouting the loudest, but often are expressing viewpoints that may make or break the issue at hand. All of these things would be demonstrated over and over in the years and challenges to come.

The power of influence

I served as BMF president from October 2003 to 2006. One of my key duties as president of the organisation was to pull our members into the bigger national discussions that the BMF was having around business leadership transformation. With the ANC having set a 50% target for women in parliament in 2002 and the BMF's display of support as seen in my appointment, I wanted to make sure the gender agenda remained a key business conversation. At the same time that I was appointed president, we as an organisation had agreed to insert into our constitution a clause that would set a gender target for elected positions in the BMF at 30%.

Although gender targets within the BMF's own leadership were long in coming and had been discussed prior to my election as president, they were by no means a fait accompli. My role as president was to keep our members updated on these discussions and to get buy-in, which I did by working through our regional chairpersons, each of whom was elected from within his or her province.

This brings up one of my first big learnings as president. Although when holding a title like president there is a perception that 'the buck stops here', in fact, with nine regional chairs, the buck actually stopped with my ability to work with and influence others. In other words, it was my job to get each regional chair to look at the organisation's interests through a broader national lens, which sometimes required asking them to put aside their provincial or individual priorities. Every BMF regional chair was a volunteer, as passionate as, if not more than I was, about our organisation's broader agenda of transformation, leadership development and vision for change. But passion can become a tension when translated into the specifics of programmes of processes of execution.

Given the ANC target of 50% in parliament, I felt 30% was not only feasible but also an important and visible demonstration to the rest of the corporate world that we at the BMF were walking our own talk. Although our members understood the importance of target-setting, people had their individual preferences. Out of nine chairpersons, two argued that we did not need to set a target, as gender representation was increasing anyway, while a few others felt 30% was too high. Negotiating the gender target clause into our constitution meant engaging each regional chairperson in order to understand why he thought the target was unnecessary or too high, and then work with him or her to canvas their constituents' votes (eight regional presidents were male, and one female represented the Western Cape).

The big lesson here was around distinguishing power from influence. You could say I held the power because I was president, but in fact my 'power' relied on the influence that I could bring to bear by engaging in a particular style with all my stakeholders – not only internally but also externally – that got their buy-in for whatever it was I wanted to achieve. In these and other debates to come, I honed my consultative leadership style, engaging with as many stakeholders as possible, and recalling my earlier work with the unions (SACCAWU) when I was a young manager at Woolworths. During my term as BMF president I learned how to work *with* people, how to work *through* people, and how to pull out and lean in on people whom I knew had unique perspectives and approaches to enhance my own.

In the end, one of the most important achievements I drove as BMF president was the addition to our constitution of the 30% gender representation in leadership target. In those days, most corporates were reluctant to even have a conversation around gender targets, and so by setting this example, the BMF took the lead on an issue that only in recent years has received serious traction as more corporates have started to talk seriously about setting targets of 30% on their boards for women. (JSE listing requirements effective 2017 call for companies to disclose and report on their policies on promotion of gender diversity.)

Skills development and training

During my term as MD, I had focused on consolidating the BMF into a more effective delivery platform for transformation and black leadership in the private sector. As president, my goal was to ensure that we gave legs to the key strategies around culture change and skills and leadership development. The sector charter conversations had helped us put flesh onto these things, and the publicity around my appointment encouraged even more open public engagement around transformation and skills development. In particular, my appointment improved the BMF's fundraising opportunities with corporates.

Having finalised the target-setting for the various sector charters, we turned our attention to asking how we would meet those targets in five and ten years. To start, we partnered with McKinsey Consulting to run a statistical projection analysing the pool of black professionals operating across the country's various industries. The analysis, which McKinsey did as part of its pro bono support of the BMF, looked to 2010, the first national milestone for achieving the sector charter targets for 2014.

McKinsey's projections clearly showed that without intervention the country would not have enough suitably qualified black professionals to fill the charter targets for professional leadership and managerial positions by 2010. Across the board, South Africa's private sector needed a renewed focus and commitment to skills development and training, and this needed to happen at a level that went beyond HR managers (who were already aware of the problem, having provided the stats in the first place). In other words, CEOs and chairs of boards needed to prioritise the skills development and training conversation.

We did two things to get that conversation started. Leveraging the private sector goodwill around my role as first female president, I engaged directly with chairmen and CEOs of listed companies about the role that we as the BMF saw business playing to ensure the successful implementation of the sector charters, which were being introduced at this time. Getting an audience with top leadership was key to progress, as so many companies left skills development with HR, which lacks the budget or authority to send people for the levels of training that were needed.

We were not talking about basic training, but leadership and executive leadership development, which carries a hefty price tag. You need serious buy-in from the top to send people on leadership development programmes like Harvard's Senior Executive Program, which at the time cost about USD$25 000. (In 1997 when I attended with a 50% scholarship from USAID, Woolworths had covered the balance.) On top of the per-person cost of good training programmes, a company needs to send at least five to ten people to make a difference to their longer-term managerial pipeline. In short, the private sector needed to commit to greater skills development and training support nationally. That support would be fundamental to meeting charter targets, as well as the broader long-term goal of true transformation and economic empowerment for black people in South Africa.

Although we were making progress by meeting with CEOs on an ad hoc basis, we needed to do more to raise awareness about the serious skills shortage that could hit South Africa's private sector if corporates did not take certain measures. Fortunately, we were presented with the perfect platform for this in 2005. Having conducted the initial 2004 statistical projection that demonstrated the skills problem, McKinsey offered us a roundtable slot at the World Economic Forum in Davos the following year.

Using this platform, we focused our discussion on the need to enrich the talent pipeline adequately with more young people (especially women); increasing the number and quality of bursaries and scholarships that companies offered to make sure people got the right training; and finally, instituting formal training programmes in companies in the mould of the one I had gone through at Woolworths. Collectively, these measures could help ensure that by the time the opportunities and vacancies became available, there would be enough black people and women with the necessary exposure, development and skills to compete for them equally. If we wanted to multiply our 2 000 black and female middle managers in the country to 20 000 by 2014, we needed to develop people in both systemic and creative ways.

Our message at Davos attracted the attention of President Mbeki, who invited us to a lunch there, which was invaluable. Fellow guests included many decision-makers and CEOs of major South African companies and we were asked to share our insights with them. This was how we ended up with an even bigger platform to further demonstrate the strategic integration between the Employment Equity Act and Skills Development Act: how companies needed to reinforce the essence of the Skills Development Act by offering more development opportunities, and how by increasing access to a breadth of programmes, companies would effectively enlarge the skills pool from which they would need to fish in the future.

That lunch resulted in the South African CEOs inviting us to contact them for meetings upon returning home. Those meetings in turn opened the door to deeper discussions about what those companies could do to address the issue of transformation, skills development and training, and ultimately resulted in numerous companies sending many of their black managers onto leadership development programmes both locally and internationally. Many of the companies we met with began sending an average of 20 people a year on high-level executive training and development programmes, a practice which continues to this day.

In addition to sending their own people for leadership training, many of the organisations we met with also offered BMF members space on their own leadership development programmes. Major institutions from business schools such as Duke University and GIBS to corporates such as Nedbank, Sasol, Standard Bank and Deloitte, to name a few, invited qualifying BMF members to participate in their in-house executive development programmes at no cost. At a value of about R100 000 per person, a free seat was of great value and benefit for our members, whose outside perspectives also added value to those in-house programmes.

Social impact agenda

During my tenure as BMF president, leadership and skills development training became a driving passion. I view the BMF's accomplishments in this area under my presidency as setting a foundation of building blocks to get the country to start meeting its broader transformation and skills development agenda. I do not claim that these efforts radically changed the country, but I do believe they helped set in motion an important process of raising awareness about the importance of skills development.

Since that time, I have made a point of 'volunteering' to support skills development and work experience initiatives led by both government and the private sector. Although the word 'volunteering' most often evokes what I call 'soul work' – the token gestures you make for personal causes like a soup kitchen or a children's home – the volunteering that I'm talking about here is the type that business leaders strategically choose based on potential to change or shift organisations or even society. In this kind of 'social impact work', you select a service or cause or organisation where your skill set and passion can have maximum impact vis-à-vis whatever change it is you seek.

As my passion is around improving access to skills, work opportunities and the economy, over the years I have volunteered my support to processes and bodies that bring different partners together to address the issue of lack of skills in critical areas in the country, and whose success comes out of their consultative and collaborative nature. To that end, I have been involved in ASGISA,[7] the SETAs[8] and the HRDC.

The Human Resource Development Council is where I have done most of my 'community work' since 2010. Chaired by the deputy president of the country, and sitting under the ministry of Higher Education and Training, the HRDC is large with about 30 people, including cabinet ministers, vice-chancellors from universities, business CEOs and the heads of different labour federations. Established in 2010, the council's mandate is to develop a strategy for building the country's human resource base to support a prosperous and inclusive society and economy. Our focus is on integrating policy and ensuring that the 'education value chain' is fixed where it is broken, and that bottlenecks in our national systems from education to the workplace and labour are cleared.

By education value chain, I mean from early education through the labour system in its entirety. To properly address this system, you start with a child ready to go to school, asking if they have childcare facilities that are appropriate to their cognitive development needs and so forth until the day they graduate. Then you look at the graduates, asking if they are getting the degrees or qualifications that allow them to operate in the economy sustainably as individuals, whether this translates into creating a company or working for someone else. Finally, you examine the availability of development programmes that help a person to improve and grow throughout his or her working career until retirement.

The beauty of the HRDC is that sitting around the table you have all the players who, at some point or another, have a role in that development life cycle. Our task is to ensure that all the relevant policies, programmes, projects, interventions and strategies are streamlined and optimised to support the larger objective around developing needed skills rather than focusing only on sectoral imperatives. When we identify an area as a blockage or dysfunctional, we can collectively talk about how best to fix it, who is best placed to fix it, and then ensure that government appropriates the resources required to do so. In other words, it allows us to think about and act on the whole value chain so that we can fix it in a way that eventually gives us a system that functions.

Our role in the HRDC as business is to contribute our understanding of the skills required by the labour market, ensuring that the skills being developed are relevant to what the market requires, both in type and quantity. The public good that comes out of senior business leaders and CEOs engaging in a space like this is clear, as it is about working with government and labour and higher education to influence, shape and change the fundamental issues that affect how education, employment and economic growth support one another. I feel blessed to have been in a position where I could play a role in this space.

With our historical lack of development and skills, and an education system that has not produced the kind or quality of skills that we require, no one company or organisation or government department or ministry will ever accomplish what is needed alone. Given the many places where the system is admittedly broken, it is vital that we continue to work collaboratively to fix it so that we can finally provide all of our people – especially black youth – with the experiences and opportunities they need to seize their own economic empowerment.

CHAPTER 9

◇◇◇◇◇◇◇◇◇◇◇◇◇

Another kind of integration

When the non-executive role of BMF president had come on the horizon for me in 2003, I realised it was time to start looking for my next executive position. Having promised Simon Susman when I left Woolworths that I would let him know when I came back on the market, I called him first. However, it quickly became clear that accepting a senior executive role at Woolworths would require relocating back to Cape Town, which was not an option. On the bright side, Woolworths invited me to join its board as a non-executive director, thus fulfilling the aspiration that I had 'dared' to entertain back when I was a graduate trainee on day one of my induction!

Once I had spread the word among my networks that I would be available for an executive role, I soon received a call from Nedbank's outgoing CEO, Richard Laubscher. I had worked closely with the Banking Council and various banks during my involvement in developing the financial sector charter, and so none of us were strangers. I met Richard in July 2003 for coffee and we discussed our mutual interests. He then invited me to have further discussions with Nedbank's incoming CEO Tom Boardman and ExCo member Derek Muller.

In December 2003 Tom invited me to join Nedbank, and by January 2004 I began my 'double-billing' as BMF (non-executive) president as well as Director of Business Transformation, Marketing and Group Strategy for

Nedbank, a position that also made me the company's first female ExCo member.

Business transformation

It was a time of major transition for everyone involved. About a year before I came on board, Nedbank had concluded a merger that brought twelve brands, including BoE, Peoples Bank, Syfrets, Natal Building Society (NBS), and Old Mutual Bank under a single umbrella. Tom Boardman had recently taken the reins as CEO and was in the process of restructuring the ExCo. This comprised an impressive group of leaders and experts in their respective fields. My new colleagues included the likes of Lot Ndlovu (former BMF president and former CEO of Peoples Bank) and Rob Shuter (current CEO of MTN).

As head of Marketing and Strategy, I was responsible for integrating and aligning the twelve merged business brands into a single new identity with a shared culture, set of values and market position. My portfolio was extremely broad, encompassing Corporate Affairs (including stakeholder engagements and community affairs), Group Strategy and Marketing. Leading the team to reposition and establish Nedbank's new brand identity and culture meant working very closely with Tom, various colleagues on the ExCo and a wide range of stakeholders across the business.

While Tom drove the external buy-in, achieving internal stakeholder buy-in for the brand merger formed the bulk of my job. This meant ensuring that everyone moved forward with a sense that they had contributed to shaping and redefining our new culture. The first stakeholder level we addressed was the business unit CEOs and senior management teams from the different companies. Each business and its senior team had passionately developed and grown its corporate identity over the years in the market and was structured differently. My task was to gather everyone under one new umbrella brand about which they could feel as passionately as they had their previous one.

PART 3: A NATIONAL STAGE

As was the case in the larger transformation journey that the country was experiencing, the journey of change that came with the merger caused some people to feel they were losing something by moving forward. Even if you demonstrate that the loss is not tangible, the emotional association with a brand and way of life can go deep for people who have built loyalty in a company over the years. We approached this challenge by co-creating a common shared value statement across the group. The aspiration was to become the 'deep green bank' – with a focus on sustainability.

Although they often seemed similar, the values of each organisation differed in nuance. For example, almost every company says that people are important to their business, but the nuances of how each company deals with its own employees differs based on its culture. On paper you may have the same value, but you have to find a common definition of what that value means to each organisation. Because of this, I was highly aware that the process of defining our new common values together would be key to their successful uptake.

We began by engaging with employees using tools such as the Barrett Survey (a highly effective way to manage and measure organisational culture) to understand and define which values resonated most deeply with all of our people. Facilitating those conversations with senior leadership and staff was a life-changing process. In those workshops, people shared their fears about changing to a new dispensation: they spoke about the ways in which their personal identities had become wrapped up in the previous brand, and how making this change to the new brand threatened them on an almost existential level.

As a facilitator or participant, you gained new insights every time you discussed the difficulties of moving to the future, a conversation which of course paralleled the discussions we were having as a country about fear of the unknown in the new South Africa. On that note, we used the opportunity of our rebranding to discuss the financial services charter (FSC) with our staff, unpacking the possibilities the FSC offered the company in terms of business benefits as well as discussing the social impact we wanted the company to have across South Africa. For example, reaching out to previously 'unbanked' lower-income customers, which both extended the bank's footprint nationally and gave people access to banking through infrastructure like ATMs and new branches in rural areas and townships.

The next critical level of stakeholder engagement was with our customers. Like the employees from the different banks and businesses, our customers were now being asked to gather under one new brand. This meant rethinking our customer value proposition. Again, Tom was very closely involved in this process, working with the different marketing teams to ensure that our market position incorporated all the different aspirations held by the entire range of customers from the different banks.

Working with my brand marketing team and the advertising agencies, the brand identity that we ultimately developed from all of these engagements was expressed through the theme of 'deep green'. We wanted to be a 'green' and caring bank that would be known as a great place to work, to bank and to invest. The deep green theme conveyed the novelty, freshness and sustainability that were intrinsic elements of our newly unified brand. Tom engaged in numerous roadshows, visiting staff across the country's different offices, accompanied by various members of the ExCo team, including myself, to directly share the vision of our new brand with all the businesses.

The value of the insider-outsider

My primary vision and ambition at Nedbank were seeing the company's new unified brand successfully articulated and embraced. The financial sector was an entirely new industry for me, however, and the need to rapidly absorb the details of how this new space functioned caused me great anxiety. Recalling my failure to pass accounting in varsity (three times!), one of the first things I had asked about my position was how much I would need to learn about accounting. Tom had assured me that the bank had plenty of accountants to crunch numbers and that I had been brought in for my sound business knowledge and understanding of how organisations operate and run.

PART 3: A NATIONAL STAGE

It turned out that my existing skills and experience stood me in good stead. At Nedbank I saw how everything from helping run my mother's businesses at an early age to my exposure to the fundamental building blocks of a business of scale at Woolworths to the leadership skills I had developed, especially in stakeholder management, as MD of the BMF were now coming to play. The lesson affirmed here was that business is business, regardless of sector or scale. At this level, it was no longer only about technical skills or the nuts and bolts of why a machine did or did not work, but rather about solid leadership and management skills, which proved transferrable from one industry to the next. Although I was coming into a new environment, I brought to the table my diverse experiences in decision-making and problem solving which, more often than not, are the key functions of management and leadership.

In those first months while I was still familiarising myself with the bank's workings, I also came to appreciate the comprehensive toolkit that the Harvard SEP course had provided me. Everything I encountered at Nedbank fit into the various components of what I had studied in that programme. From management systems to business processes to finance, my global understanding of how a business operates rested on that sound foundation. This is in part why business school education offers so much value, whether a short programme or a year's MBA (the other key benefit being the peer network gained). The classic business school framework of applied learning will always prove useful as you grow in your career, and the principles and fundamentals of how businesses run and how organisations are built provide an excellent base from which to operate.

◇◇◇◇◇

Although initially appearing as a hurdle to overcome, my 'outsider' status proved in many ways to be an advantage. Unencumbered by the baggage that some of the merged entities laboured under, my fresh perspective often positively served our team dynamic. The only outside person on the ExCo, I could ask questions or analyse processes without raising people's defences, which sometimes helped the team to move faster on certain issues.

For example, when the time came to determine the enterprise-wide information management system to be used by the one Nedbank group, we considered each organisation's system and process, with the intent of pulling them together and deciding which was most appropriate. Even though we worked with consultants, as a member of the ExCo, my 'objective' outsider view was particularly prized, mainly because I was not attached to any specific system. I facilitated the conversation by asking logical questions and sometimes prefacing my queries with statements like: 'This may be an obvious question for you, but ...' or 'Because I am new in this sector or industry, can you explain how this works or why we are doing that?' The disarming nature of such statements, especially when coming from a sincere place, can be highly effective.

All that said, I still felt a huge pressure to get up to speed and contribute positively as an informed team member in as short a space of time as possible. Nedbank was a big stage, and failing here would be to fail spectacularly, so this was a prime anxiety. There were complex aspects of the industry – things such as how the balance sheet of a bank works, or what security you needed with the Reserve Bank and how that governance and regulator relationship works – that were fundamental to developing strategy, operations and fiscal sustainability. I raised this concern with Tom on day one, who appointed Derek Muller, a fellow ExCo member who had been with the bank for over 25 years, as my formal mentor. Sitting with Derek after an ExCo meeting and being able to talk through the intricacies of what had been presented was invaluable.

The lesson here was that when entering any new environment, regardless of whether it is an unfamiliar industry or one you know well, you must always ask questions. The detrimental belief that one should know 'everything' at the senior level can prevent people from doing this. Although I was a senior executive, asking questions for clarity and understanding and requesting one-on-one tutorials were what enabled me to contribute fully at Nedbank. This approach has never let me down.

The stretch assignment

Working in an entirely new industry at Nedbank while also serving as BMF president was a true stretch assignment. It also gave me unique and valuable perspectives on the challenges of meeting transformation targets from inside a large business at the executive level. Tom and I had many conversations about the broader issues of change and transformation in South Africa, talks that were extremely valuable for me given that I was simultaneously serving as president of the BMF, where we engaged with similar questions of business and transformation, but from the perspective of advocating for black business leaders and managers.

An example of a situation where straddling these two worlds provided perspectives valuable to how I functioned in both was the bank's own target-setting process. While the ownership equity element was established by the financial sector charter at 10%, the bank was responsible for setting its own employment equity diversity targets. As BMF president I obviously wanted Nedbank to be ambitious in its diversity goals. But reviewing the existing baselines of black professionals for different positions – for example, saying we needed so many actuarial scientists by such-and-such a date – it quickly became obvious that external interventions had to be taken to achieve those targets. This led to numerous discussions amongst the ExCo and with Tom about the role we as Nedbank should be playing to develop the talent pipeline – conversations that enriched my understanding as BMF president concerning the meaningful and practical things we needed to do as a country and with the private sector to see our transformation targets met.

Another thing I realised at this time was that although the barriers to achieving our talent needs in the technical levels were largely about training pipelines, the barriers at senior management levels were much more about political will. That is, the need for leadership to decide it wants to make the move to embrace the culture change that allows real transformation to take place. This was expressed in so many ways. For example, when considering a black or female candidate for a senior role, executives often invoked the 'risk' involved in this appointment. However, if the person was a white male, the language shifted to talking about offering the person a 'stretch opportunity' to grow. When political will is lacking and transformation is seen as an issue of (begrudging) compliance, diversity candidates will be identified as 'risk' appointments. Not surprisingly, support and mentorship for that individual comes through in a similarly begrudging fashion. On the flip-side, when leadership has the political will for culture change, the language of 'stretch' and 'opportunity' comes into play.

My own career is an example of this. Looking at my journey I have to ask: how was I able to go into the financial services environment (or later the energy petrochemical sector) with no prior experience and still be successful? It was not because I was so special, but rather because the political will from the CEOs and the board of directors and other people in decision-making positions provided me the mentorship and support that I needed to succeed. In other words, I was given stretch opportunities, rather than seen as a risk appointment. My trajectory causes me to question the so-called skills shortage when considering the senior executive levels, as these levels are no longer about technical competence (because at these levels that is a given), but rather about providing the stretch assignments and necessary rotations so that people are ready to seize that next leadership role. When it comes to not bringing black people or women up into executive positions, we have to ask if there is a deliberate lack of will to make it work.

Personal transformations

With my secondment to the BMF in 2000, Phila and I had moved to Joburg, joining Presto, who had been based there since 1997. Although one might think that ending our 'commuting family' arrangement would make things easier, in fact there were challenges around re-establishing a rhythm with all of us finally living in the same city. Presto was thriving in his career as a general manager within the Transnet groups, and I was constantly travelling to meetings, conferences and seminars with the BMF. When it became clear that I would likely become BMF president and participate even more intimately in the national dialogue on South Africa's transformation journey while also joining Nedbank as a senior executive, we had to acknowledge that we were essentially living separate lives.

The breakdown of a marriage is, invariably, perceived as a public failure regardless of how you look at it. This is often because there are other players invested in that relationship. It may be children, family members, adoring public or just fodder for the press. It is also true that some people overstay in their relationships because they just can't deal with the 'public' fallout that goes with their trauma of separation. The vested players – family, friends and colleagues – are also sucked into this drama. No one in your close circle is left untouched.

Ironically, Presto, who was previously my greatest champion from a career perspective, found it difficult to deal with the confident and focused woman I had become. The metamorphosis that had begun to happen during our professional and physical distances became starkly evident. My professional trajectory was faster and more visible than Presto's and the strain was becoming increasingly clear, especially when my corporate climb seemed imminent. We had met when I was only eighteen years old and got married when I was 21. Along the way I had transformed into a woman my husband no longer recognised.

In 2003, after seventeen years of marriage, Presto and I divorced.

What pulled me out of the shock of divorce was the fact that my friends and family members, from both the Njoli and Fakude families, supported me through the pain. My sisters-in-law, in particular, (Sis Masesi Gumbi Msimango and Sis Martha Makhubu) showed me great solidarity. I remember Sis Masesi insisting a month after I had moved to my new place, that they wanted to come and see that Phila and I were okay. Her kind insistence was that they had been part of the delegation that had travelled to my home in Stutterheim, to pay lobola, and had promised my mother that they would look after me as if I were their own sister. They wanted to honour this promise, specifically for the sake of my son, so he would always know that he still had his Fakude family regardless of the status of his parents' relationship. This was a powerful vindication and endorsement of the lobola tradition of our culture. Thirty-three years on since that traditional wedding, these two women, whom I still consider my older sisters, made me realise that I could never forget the stand they took within their family in the midst of great challenges they faced. In retrospect, though not spoken in those terms, they were true feminists in their own right. They stood for the sisterhood that defied blood.

Phila was in boarding school at the time of the divorce and so didn't feel the impact as much as he would have had he lived at home, although I'm sure it worried him. Both before and after the divorce, I tried to be available as much as possible for the important events in my son's life, but every now and then telling moments made me pause.

One of these moments occurred after our divorce when I was at Nedbank. Phila had had a small accident at school playing rugby – he had bitten his lip and needed to be stitched up. Trying to call both of us immediately, the housemaster managed to get hold of Presto first, and he had gone to fetch Phila. Returning home as soon as I could, I arrived to find Phila happily watching TV. After an hour or so of fussing around, I realised I could still make a 3pm meeting I had called. When I asked Presto if it was fine for me to go back, he did a bit of a double take, but then agreed. I asked Phila, who was engrossed in whatever he was watching on TV, if it was okay for me to go.

'Yeah, it's fine,' he said.

'Are you sure?'

'Yes, Mom, of course. I'm fine. Just go.' Obviously, I was disturbing his TV viewing.

Having got my son's permission, I grabbed my things to leave but as I was closing the door, I heard him say, 'Hey, Mom, thanks for coming.'

I got into my car, and started to reverse, all the time thinking, No! This is too much. My son should not be thanking me for coming to see if he is okay. I stopped the car and went back inside.

'Why did you say that?' I asked Phila.

'It's just that I know you had to come out of work,' he said, almost apologetic and clearly surprised to see me back.

Although I always made a big point of being sure that I had Phila 'covered', at that moment it really hit me that maybe I was not as conscious as I thought. Then again, I had a co-parent who was as committed, if not more so, than I, so why did I feel badly when I knew Phila's father was there? If the situation were reversed, would a father feel this way? Logically I knew Phila was fine, but sometimes these things are not about logic. This is where the difficulty comes and the soul searching happens, because you never know if you are getting it right.

In my case, it truly 'took a village' to raise my son. I will always be grateful to all the people who helped me to raise Phila, from his nanny MamCirha, to my mother, who stepped in elegantly, uprooting herself from the Eastern Cape to the Western Cape to 'au pair' her grandchild when he was eight years old and seriously needed his grandmother. I also had sister-friends in Cape Town and later in Johannesburg who became Phila's special mothers, and last but not least, Bongiwe Chipape, our housekeeper, who provided us both with stability and has kept warmth in our home for close to two decades.

Truth be told, 20 years ago I envied my male colleagues for having wives who helped and supported their careers by anchoring their homes and families. Often the lament from my female peers with children was how much they wished they also had 'wives' to help shoulder the parenting burden and challenge. Fortunately, parenting is a lifelong lesson and journey. One of the greatest joys in my life has been parenting Phila and being parented by him in return. Children ground you, requiring you to be honest and consistent. You can't say one thing today and do something else tomorrow, as they will always challenge you. My son knew that I was always busy at work, he accepted it as fact and has never judged me for it. I therefore needed to give myself the permission to do what I thought best for my career. As a parent the learning never ceases, and hopefully some of those lessons help you to become a better person and a better leader – that is, someone who is both in touch with the next generation and also has real stakes in the future.

CHAPTER 10

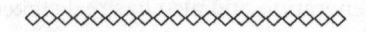

Preparing to fly

It was in the period of my transitioning from being a married woman to a single woman that I became the president of the BMF. That same eventful year I turned 40. For the first time I felt certified as an independent adult in the truest sense of the word. As if to add insult to injury, when I tried to change my surname back to my maiden name, people would congratulate me thinking I had either got married or remarried. Attempting to explain what had just happened usually brought me tears and so I made a conscious decision to abandon that particular transition and retain my married name. After all, I had been a Fakude long enough to be their child in all respects – even the ancestors knew that. It was also critical for me that I reclaim the name as my own because my professional career had been attached to it. And that's what I chose to do.

Only fourteen months after beginning my job at Nedbank, I received a call from a head hunter. This was a normal occurrence, and I automatically said I was neither available nor looking to move. He was quite persistent, however, and a few days later called again, saying he had shared my refusal with his client, who asked that I at least give their proposal a hearing. He shared a few more details about the position, which reported directly to the CEO of a top listed company operating in over 30 countries.

'That does sound interesting,' I conceded. I asked who the client was.

'I'm not sure I can disclose that,' he replied.

'Well, that doesn't help me, because I'm not actually looking to change and am happy where I am,' I said.

I thought that would be the end of it but a few days later he called again.

'The client is Sasol,' he informed me.

'In that case the answer is definitely no,' I responded.

South Africa's largest petrochemical company, Sasol, had begun the process of applying to be listed on the New York Stock Exchange about eighteen months earlier. In response to standard application questions around risks in its countries of operation, Sasol had identified BEE. This happened as momentum was building around employment equity and BEE and we – meaning the country's major black business associations along with government – had broadly identified key industries in the economy that should drive transformation in terms of ensuring that black players were brought in both to the ownership (BEE ownership) and management (CEO and executive) spaces. Both liquid fuel and mining – Sasol's core businesses – were among the key sectors identified (others were the broader financial services sector and ICT).

Having competent black people in the right positions at the right level was a widespread and legitimate business concern. However, the negative controversy around Sasol's public position came down to its attitude and apparent lack of will. By contrast, two other companies seeking listing at the same time as Sasol had answered the risk question by seeing the risk in *not* embracing BEE. The fact that Sasol had come out and publicly affirmed its view of BEE as risky did not bode well in terms of its leadership's will to transform. Sasol's statement triggered a national debate about BEE, with no less than the president of the country, Thabo Mbeki, writing an open letter to Sasol's board.

As BMF president I also weighed in, calling out Sasol's chairman for being short-sighted, which he was. His role was to be visionary, yet he was refusing to acknowledge that transformation was the future.

The debate became an embarrassment for the company, highlighting its misalignment with the nation's foremost strategy, and leading to employees, investors and other stakeholders questioning Sasol's ability to align itself with the country's broader agenda of transformation. Shortly before the head hunter first contacted me, Sasol had appointed Pat Davies as its new CEO and Trevor Munday as deputy CEO and CFO. Soon thereafter, they both made a public commitment to transform the company.

Despite my continued rejection of its job offer (the irony of Sasol's decision to appoint two white males to its top two positions was not lost on anyone), Sasol continued to request meetings with me as BMF president (as well as with others like me) to help it address its institutional challenge. In that spirit, I engaged in discussions with Pat and Trevor, often bringing the MD of BMF, Jerry Vilakazi, with me. I found it encouraging that Sasol's new leadership was seeking these conversations, and that Pat and Trevor so clearly realised that the company was in trouble around this issue. As we continued to engage, I saw that they understood that resisting change would bring bigger challenges and even a backlash that could impact their licence to operate in South Africa and beyond. Sasol had begun to enter other African and Middle Eastern countries, and its leaders understood the need proactively to sort out its value systems and culture to embrace diversity and inclusion, regardless of geographic location. Although perhaps exaggerated in our country, problems of diversity and inclusion were by no means uniquely South African, and the same fundamental issues were increasingly relevant across the globalised landscape.

As it became apparent that Sasol's leadership was still 'courting' me, I made my agenda as transparent as possible; that is, to drive culture change and transformation in South Africa's private sector regardless of whom I was employed by. Over the next six months we engaged in what was a kind of reverse interviewing process, during which time Pat and Trevor came to convince me that the company's top leadership had truly bought in to the work that needed to be done. This was crucial, because if I joined Sasol, I needed to be sure I had full support from that leadership and there were no misunderstandings about the need or methods required for culture change and transformation.

And so I started to take the idea seriously. I consulted external mentors and BMF colleagues alike – people such as Max Sisulu (a former Sasol director), Bheki Sibiya, Eric Mafuna and Jerry Vilakazi – outlining the challenges and asking whether I should even consider the job. After all, the banks were also a key transformation sector, and I was making good progress at Nedbank and loving the leadership of Tom Boardman.

Almost across the board, the response I got was why was I even asking. As the country's largest corporate taxpayer, Sasol represented an enormous opportunity for transformation if its leadership was truly ready to make the necessary moves. After numerous private discussions with Pat, I was convinced of the company's intellectual and emotional commitment to the need for change. It was because of this bigger national agenda that my stay at Nedbank was cut short. Tom gave me his blessing to move on.

Accepting this transformation project at a top ten listed company that was visibly struggling in the public space around its role as a corporate leader had one major downside: it required stepping down from a second term as BMF president. I knew I could not do justice to both jobs at the same time. Not going for a second term at the BMF remains the hardest decision I have had to take in my career.

Some of my BMF associates and stakeholders urged me to stay, insisting that my work to reposition the organisation as a relevant and strategic national partner and thought leader needed more time. The ground we had gained after the WEF in terms of getting corporate leaders on board with skills development training remained incredibly important to me, and for some time I had a conflict in my heart about stepping down. I also dearly would have liked to have seen another woman take over from me, yet there was no clear candidate to assume that legacy.

In the end I was able to go because I felt I had achieved what I had set out to do at the BMF. On top of this, the possibility of delivering the transformation agenda at a business of Sasol's scale was equally if not more important than the work I could do at the BMF. My goal for Sasol was nothing less than a visible demonstration of how a global corporate organisation can change and transform in the face of great scepticism, internally, nationally and internationally. The BMF needed to remain independent and neutral, which position might have been difficult to maintain under a president employed by a company with Sasol's publicly stated challenges. And so I made my choice.

Legacies

It is widely accepted that succession planning is a very important process for any institution or organisation. It contributes greatly to stability and maintaining of momentum in terms of your key strategies. Throughout its existence the BMF as an organisation has always managed this process in the most intellectual and elegant fashion. It looks at the external environment to gauge the political and social climate before embarking on the elections for the top leadership positions. This is done to establish that the 'right' leader is matched with the challenges of the day.

In the four previous presidential elections, the MD succeeded the president. For instance, when Professor Wiseman Nkuhlu was the BMF's president (number 6), the MD was Lot Ndlovu; then Lot became the president (number 7), and Bheki Sibiya was his MD; I was the MD under Bheki's presidency (number 8).

Later, when I became president (number 9), Jerry Vilakazi was the MD. However, because I had been uncertain about running for a second presidential term, the succession for the next president was not as smooth as usual. My indecisiveness created a vacuum for uncertainty in the leadership transition.

Two years into my presidency, unbeknown to me, my deputy, Mzwanele Manyi, was already canvassing members for his nomination to become the next president of the organisation. Somehow he had managed to push forward a position to the members that even if I had wanted to continue with the next term of office, he felt that my leadership style of 'quiet diplomacy' (or 'boardroom diplomacy', as he referred to it) with corporates was not suitable for the radical economic transformation that was required at the time. As much as I would have agreed with this sentiment had we openly discussed it within the BMF, as we normally did on policy issues, what was disappointing was that he had never previously raised this approach with me. The reason he sought to unseat me, as we would soon discover, was that I was perceived to be a 'Thabo Mbeki person'. His chauvinistic political views made him argue that my 'feminine' leadership style was not radical enough; the sub-text, however, as we were soon to understand, was that the BMF had been 'mortgaged' as part of the Polokwane/ANC Conference struggle. Manyi had nailed his colours to the Zuma mast in the leadership race for the presidency of the ANC against Mbeki. He had promised to bring the 'black professional' vote with him – such were the politics of the day. In my political naivety, and my perceived vacillation regarding holding the BMF presidency as well as taking on the Sasol transformation challenge, I had allowed the organisation to 'flounder' through an election process that would have been unnecessary had we openly discussed succession early enough, thus playing right into the hands of those opposed to gender equality. One of the lessons to be learned here, and one that I painfully took on board, is that ambivalence is not good for an organisation.

Over the years, I have felt very sad about that situation. I regret that I let so many people in the organisation down at the time by not managing the succession process as proactively as I could have done. Thankfully, institutions like the BMF are much more resilient than we can imagine and today, fifteen years later, the BMF is still thriving and will soon be celebrating 45 years of existence.

Mzwanele Manyi became my successor as BMF president. In 2007 he was quoted in the media as saying that South Africa's skills shortage was an 'urban legend'.[9] Although he had his reasons for making this claim (one of his arguments was that racist companies that did not want to appoint black people hid behind the skills shortage issue), the reality was that as a country we still lacked the depth and breadth of skills required. The outright denial of this need that I had championed heralded a sea change in an organisation I had grown up in and held dear. It also made for controversial headlines.

Having worked closely with Manyi for years, it was difficult not to take this personally. My initial upset gave way, however, and I realised that rather than sitting and sulking over it I needed to confront the issue openly. To that end, I called Manyi to discuss the matter.

'The way you've positioned the issue will have unintended consequences,' I said, referring to the fact that it was a free pass from the BMF for companies to abandon development and training responsibilities, which already fell short of what was required.

Manyi defended his position, but we continued to disagree. To his credit Manyi invited me to participate in a panel conference about the 'myth' of the skills shortage in South Africa. The panel, which included academics and politicians, created a context for people to understand the structural and historic reasons for South Africa's skills shortage. I personally used the panel to express my deeply held belief that whatever the reasons for the shortage, it remained a crippling reality, and as South Africans, it was vital that we dealt with it constructively rather than waste energy debating or denying its existence.

Unfortunately, the skills shortage matter was not the only issue I happened to disagree with Manyi on as new president of the BMF. Although publicly contradicting Manyi was unpleasant and put me in the media to a degree that I found highly uncomfortable, the lesson here was that engagement will always yield a better outcome than resentment.

Throughout my career I have been incredibly fortunate in that most of the processes I have engaged in have aligned with my principles and value system. When facing moral dilemmas in business – including whether or not to speak out about something – the standard I employ is whether or not I can defend the action to my family and my son. In the case of this debate, I also was heartened to see that I was not alone in responding to the issue. Adding my voice to the many others who both directly and indirectly confronted the BMF on this issue had the positive result of putting skills development back on the agenda.

Numerous leadership lessons came out of this incident. First, the reinforcement of the need for buy-in. As a leader you must ensure that you are not pushing processes, policies or strategies alone, but that you have buy-in from others who will protect the legacy because they also own it. Second, the value of never burning bridges for any reason. Although you may disagree with an individual or an entire organisation that you have been associated with, burning bridges over those disagreements never benefits anyone. Someday in the future that organisation may want to engage with you, but if you have made a big point of severing the relationship on a sour note, it makes such future engagements uncomfortable or often impossible. Even if things are not working, you should always leave gracefully when you move on. The last lesson was around knowing when to walk away. As a leader your term comes to an end, and once you are gone you cannot continue to manage 'from the grave'. When your turn is over, you must walk away.

I do feel the need to add that now, well over ten years since that discussion, the skills shortage in critical sectors remains one of our country's key pressing challenges. It is informed by different issues – from the dysfunction of our basic education system to the lack of in-service training and internship opportunities in South African businesses for graduates to gain the experience they need to operate fully and effectively. As companies and industries, we need to spend more money and effort to develop young people and offer them opportunities for exposure, especially to technical and hard skills. Until we fulfil this imperative, we will continue to limp along as a country when it comes to growing the economy and meeting the employment requirements of our population. When corporates still continue to 'look surprised' 25 years later by the lack of skills in the country, I wonder who they think was supposed to upskill the labour force?

PART 4

GLOBAL TRANSFORMATIONS

If the organisational transformation is to be successful, all individuals in the leadership team must be willing to take a hard look at their own personal values and behaviours and make the adjustments that are necessary to embrace the new culture. Organisations don't transform. People do! Without this personal commitment, cultural change will not happen.

RICHARD BARRETT

From *Liberating the Corporate Soul: Building a Visionary Organisation*

CHAPTER 11

◇◇◇◇◇◇◇◇◇◇◇◇◇◇◇◇

Awakening a South African giant

In October 2005 I stepped into the role of executive director of Strategy and Human Resources at Sasol. A company established in order to develop the energy independence that allowed the apartheid government to beat economic oil sanctions, Sasol in many ways still struck me as an institution that embodied pre-1994 South Africa. With its white male leadership and much publicised resistance to change, this industrial giant reflected the reality that although politically things might have changed, South Africa's economy was still controlled and owned by a white minority.

I've long viewed business as a microcosm of society, and so I was highly aware that it was against this backdrop that I was to develop the strategy to reposition Sasol into a committed corporate citizen and willing player in the new South Africa's economic transformation. As such my goal was not only to shift the culture of this particular company with its particular history, but also to develop a process that could be replicated across corporate South Africa.

As mentioned, the debates triggered the previous year by Sasol's unenthusiastic position vis-à-vis BEE had resulted in its board appointing a new executive team, led by new CEO Pat Davies, an engineer and strategist who for 31 years had guided the company's oil and gas exploration business to its now global status. Under Pat's leadership, the company had begun its process

PART 4: GLOBAL TRANSFORMATIONS

of soul searching. By the time I arrived six months later, a full set of perception surveys with key internal and external stakeholders had been conducted.

Equipped with these survey results, which deeply explored people's experiences of the organisation, I started my own process of observing and assessing the culture. What I found was an intensely IQ-based culture defined by high-performance ideals. With no shortage of internationally recognised scientists and engineers doing cutting-edge research, Sasol was a company that prized intellectual prowess above all else. Many of Sasol's people had worked together for years. A surprisingly large number had received Sasol bursaries and thus been with the company since university, and a fair number had met their spouses there. The resulting environment was one in which people's loyalty to the organisation was almost familial in quality. Most of the Sasol employees were also extremely out of touch with life outside the industrial towns of Secunda and Sasolburg, where the main plants were located. This was evidenced in initial workshops, where much confusion was expressed over the negative perceptions from external stakeholders regarding the company's status as a good citizen. 'We pay our taxes, we do corporate social responsibility programmes. Why are people on our case?' was the general attitude.

With this insularity, loyalty and intellectual might came a deep arrogance and disregard for contrasting views. The attitude was: we are the best, the biggest, and always know what to do. This outlook coloured external relationships with customers, suppliers and stakeholders, perpetuating and enhancing the perception of Sasol as remote from what was happening in the country at large. It soon became clear to us that changing Sasol's culture to one that was more inclusive and open to diversity was not a challenge restricted to issues of race and gender. The organisation's combination of intellectual arrogance and unquestioning loyalty had nurtured a superiority complex that allowed the company to feel it was 'above' addressing or even acknowledging concerns of diversity. In other words, diversity of thought was not even tolerated, much less that of race or gender.

With our work cut out for us, I had in mind three key strategic areas:

The first was talent management. In an organisation that was largely white and male, with much of the upper echelons being white males over 50 years of age, succession planning that viewed diversity as a critical factor became a priority.

The second area concerned effecting a culture change in the organisation. I saw it as essential that mindset shifts be brought about so that we could create an environment where a diversity of people would feel equally represented, where they could thrive and operate at their full potential. The overriding challenge, which spoke to the prevailing shape and complexion of Sasol, was to demonstrate the increased value this strategy would bring to the organisation.

The third strategic goal spoke to the broader issue of transformation in the country at large. Sasol was out of step with what was happening in South Africa at that time; not only was it falling behind and being criticised for it – the attitude was one of hurt surprise at the criticism than acknowledgement of what needed to be done internally. Sasol was a successful entity; it had grown and expanded and delivered economically. It was a good place to work and the benefits were generous. That it had been able to do all these things as a result of an imbalance of privilege and opportunity was less acknowledged or recognised. What we needed urgently to achieve was to get Sasol plugged in to the broader transformation programme taking place in all areas of strategic development in SA, not because they needed politically to be on board but because of the increased value that would result.

About a year after I arrived, I made my first presentation to the company's top 1 000 leaders. 'I've found an organisation of warm hearts but cold hands,' I began. I then went on to explain that I had found Sasol's people as individuals to be warm, loyal and fiercely proud of their company and its achievements. However, as a group they handled external relationships with a harsh and arrogant 'command and control' attitude, which failed to translate that individual humanity. Addressing this disconnect, I concluded: 'Our challenge is to connect the head and the heart, to translate the heart's warmth to the head, and to warm the hands.'

As the company had already acknowledged the need for culture change through the surveys conducted, our conversations launched straight into what *kind* of shift could transform the culture of command and control and arrogance into a culture of inclusiveness and acknowledgement of others. In other words, to transform the win-lose attitude to one that was win-win; to shift from an environment where a lack of diversity was the order of the day, to one where diversity was encouraged and embraced. Transforming Sasol into a committed corporate citizen would require an institutional shift as profound as any we had seen so far in our new democracy. The leaders of the organisation had to drive this change.

Interventions

Having surveyed existing perceptions and outlined the principles behind the desired culture change, it was time to get to the interventions. There are a few non-negotiables to successfully implementing a culture change. First, as I have already noted, visible support from the CEO and top leadership are absolutely vital. Without this I would never have embarked on this journey. Second, a credible rationale for change beyond it being the 'right' thing is needed for employee buy-in. In the business world, matters of culture are often viewed as 'soft' strategies and are often difficult to quantify against the bottom line. Sasol was high performing and financially successful, so we needed to sell the culture change process to the organisation in language that resonated.

For Sasol, the business case for change came down to the company's growth ambitions and aspirations. Already operating in 35 countries, the company was looking ever outward, especially to the Middle East and the rest of the African continent. Continued expansion to international markets meant an increasing need to open up the organisational culture. Sustainability in our growth context required addressing concerns around diversity both within and outside South Africa, and culture change was an enabling strategy to ensure that sustainability.

Unlocking this strategy largely came down to attracting the right people and entering into healthy win-win relationships with all stakeholders, including governments. Continued growth would demand better management of our talent pipeline, and also that management needed to reflect the progressive and inclusive culture that we wanted for our company. Diversity here extended from diversity in skills and thinking to diversity in geography, race and gender. In those days we were in the early stages of establishing new projects around Africa (Mozambique) and the Middle East (Qatar), and were about to enter the employment phase of those operations. We wanted our employee value proposition in any given market to attract the right people who could bolster our brand. A reputation as a company with issues around diversity and where people of colour felt excluded was not going to draw progressive talent. In other words, our successful growth and expansion relied in part on nurturing a diverse and inclusive culture. Our next step was to create that culture.

⋄⋄⋄⋄⋄

Culture change starts with identifying the paradigm shifts that need to take place within an organisation, and then taking big symbolic actions that convey and transmit those shifts to the company. The term 'symbolic' should not be confused with meaningless or empty; it refers rather to actions that intentionally make a big and visible public statement.

The first paradigm shift we wanted to make clear at Sasol was around the face of leadership, and the first symbolic action here was my appointment as a black African woman in an executive director role. I was parachuted down into the midst of a white (Afrikaner) male-dominated management committee, neither an engineer nor a scientist, and quite frankly with little knowledge of the business or organisation. What I did bring, however, was my unique perspective gleaned from fifteen years of experience implementing new systems, integrating brands and working for culture change and business transformation at the BMF, Woolworths and Nedbank.

Appointing a single black person to the ExCom obviously was not enough, however, and Pat and Trevor agreed that within six months Sasol would hire additional black executives to the organisation's top ranks. Thus five months later, Christine Ramon, one of the youngest CFOs on a JSE-listed company became Sasol's first black CFO, and soon after, Bennie Mokaba from Shell SA joined us as executive director for Mining and Energy Operations. The conscious recruitment of black people for senior leadership positions shifted the Sasol paradigm that had said getting to the top of this organisation means being male, white (preferably Afrikaans), and an engineer or scientist. With only four executive directors at the time, Sasol had within twelve months boldly transformed the face of its ExCo from being 100% white male to 75% black and 50% female. With these changes in place, Trevor Munday retired.

Two additional 'symbolic' actions were announced within that first year. The first was around the long-standing tradition that the CEO would become chairman of the board upon retirement. Pat announced his intention to forego that tradition (he was set to retire in 2010), explaining that instead he would ask the board to appoint someone who better reflected our transformation agenda. Hixonia Nyasulu was appointed. She would serve as the first woman and black chairperson of Sasol. The second announcement heralded a paradigm shift around ownership. With plans to sell 10% of the company to as many black shareholders as possible, Sasol's board had committed to becoming the first major South African company to transfer ownership under BEE at such a scale, with an equity stake value of R26 billion.

◇◇◇◇◇

After paradigm shifts and symbolic actions comes the nitty gritty of embedding culture change throughout the organisation. Although culture change is something that has to work at every level, it rests on tenacious leadership, and so here we focused on the next layer on top – key management.

Working with the top 2 500 people across our organisation of 35 000 employees, we launched 'Project Enterprise', a values-driven leadership programme the primary intent of which was to shift the company's culture. These days 'values-driven leadership' is a buzzword phrase, but back then it was not so well embraced. Our first task then was to define values-driven leadership: what did it mean and how could we get our top layer of leadership to buy into it?

We ran a values survey (using the same Barrett tool that had served us so well at Nedbank) with our top 2 500 people, asking what values they currently saw exhibited in the organisation, what values they felt the organisation should aspire to have, and what values they personally embraced. A team of about 30 people – all senior business executives – led all aspects of Project Enterprise. The decision to use our brightest high-potential young leaders to drive the programme rather than HR staff further underscored the importance top leadership was placing on this culture change, making its connection to the organisation's future as clear and visible as possible.

Over the course of the eighteen months from mid-2006 to early 2008, the company's top 2 500 people across all divisions participated in two-day workshops. With working groups of about 20, these 2 500 leaders helped redefine the company's values, their own participation also securing their buy-in to the process. Workshops followed an 'inside out' methodology: starting with people's personal values, facilitators asked them to reflect on who they were and how their behaviour affected the organisation. These personal discussions led to discussions around the kinds of values they saw functioning in the organisation, as well as the values they would like to see. All of that finally led to conversations about the kind of culture that people believed would support the values they aspired to, which in turn led to conversations about the kinds of behaviours people thought leadership should exhibit and role model to help this new culture emerge.

Disconnects between reality and aspiration were exposed, as were those between people's personal values and values they felt the company should have. Those mismatches often led to some of the deeper conversations (for example, 'Why would you personally value kindness or integrity or respect, but not see that as an important value in the business, especially in how you deal with people who are different from you?'). The point was to make people see how values are both the glue that holds an organisation together and part of a company's DNA, affecting everything that it does and the way it is done.

Examining all the values that came up in these discussions – the current values exhibited, those we should aspire to and personal values – people then voted for their top ten. Themes began to emerge: people wanted to work in a safe environment, a high performing environment, an environment where diversity and inclusivity were embraced. In the end about fifteen values consistently came up. From those fifteen, we then prioritised the company's top five values that we would work towards embedding across the organisation. These were: safety, integrity, continuous improvement, winning with people, and customer satisfaction. Consultants like McKinsey, Mandate Molefi, and people from the Barrett Survey assisted both with the workshops and the processing of results. It was an exhaustive, comprehensive and iterative process, and the company did not skimp on the resources, time or commitment required to run it properly.

While the values conversations and workshops guided the macro-process of culture change at Sasol, we also needed to attend to micro-level interventions that people could use in the day to day. Those same workshops were used to develop and share a common language that helped people express themselves appropriately when discussing the often sensitive issues around diversity and inclusion. For example, if you felt you might say something wrong, you could say you needed to push the 'pause button', which meant needing to think before you speak. Or if you felt you needed to think more clearly about something, you'd say you wanted to 'get on the balcony' (or you could suggest that someone else might benefit from getting on the balcony or pushing the pause button).

At ExCo we also developed a set of symbols to express praise or criticism. Sasol's culture was not one where people were in the habit of praising a job well done, so finding neutral symbols to express approbation or censure around the inherently touchy topic of transformation was helpful. For example, if you did something that aligned positively to the new values, your manager might 'give you a rhino'. For a time, all the ExCo kept in our offices these little wax carvings of rhinos and elephants, which we gave out either as a form of positive acknowledgement or when something negative needed to be discussed. If you referred to an elephant in the room (or actually gave someone an elephant), this meant you needed to talk. The person could then ask, 'Is it a big or small elephant?' This shared language and set of symbols helped start uncomfortable conversations, allowing people to speak more openly and constructively.

Uncomfortable conversations

Difficult and uncomfortable conversations were part of the landscape, however, one of the most discomfiting topics was perceived racial discrimination between black and white employees when it came to how they passed through our talent pipeline. As executive director of Strategy and HR, it fell to me to ensure that whether talking about internal promotions or recruiting new hires, our talent management processes aligned with our new desired culture.

To start, we needed to redefine Sasol's ideal employee in light of the company's culture change aspirations. To do this, my HR team used the Barrett Survey outcomes to articulate the preferred qualities connected both to our existing staff as well as new hires, focusing in particular on 'competencies of the future', or the qualities needed to expand our business in diverse markets. We identified three primary desired qualities: ability to influence, empathy and resilience. Ability to influence, because successfully selling your reason for doing something is more productive than charging in and demanding it. Empathy, because embracing diversity requires the ability and desire to understand people who differ from you; to literally put yourself in their shoes. And resilience, because working in new environments and situations requires the ability to bounce back regardless of challenges.

Next we needed to examine how senior promotions and development opportunities were being distributed. In the interest of linking our talent management and culture change processes with our overall strategy for diversity, the group ExCo decided to rotate individuals from senior management across the business on a deliberate and systematic basis. Rotation at this level is either a promotion or a lateral move that gives someone the opportunity to experience a different aspect of the business. Either way, the benefit for the individual is exposure to another sector, new skills and preparation for future promotions. We made it standard practice in our talent management process to look at business rotations twice a year (rather than on an ad hoc basis, as had previously been the norm), and also to consider how well an individual was driving the new values and living the culture when selecting candidates for rotation or promotion.

We constantly had to monitor and challenge nominations that were put forward for such opportunities. Many of these conversations represented the very first instance a challenge based on diversity had been made at this level, and they were very uncomfortable at the start. Most often the issue at hand was not about the individual's technical competence and performance, but rather that their leadership style did not adequately reflect the new cultural values we were promoting. People had their protégés whom they had mentored and earmarked, and when those nominations were challenged for these reasons, it could spark real sensitivities, forcing robust discussions around why this one was unacceptable and not that one. In an organisation previously so insulated, these were really painful discussions for many to have, and using the mirror analogy we would encourage the individual to deeply reflect on the feedback by 'looking in the mirror'.

Support from our CEO Pat Davies was vital here. The first time (2007) we undertook a major job rotation with senior executives to introduce them to different business areas as part of their personal development, it was necessary for Pat and myself to hold the line in terms of promoting and appointing people based on Sasol's full competence framework, which now included values-driven leadership. We also helped people by making sure that where the assessment process had identified gaps, coaches and mentors were there to help them improve. This was how over the years, talent management, succession planning and identifying the future leaders of the organisation became inextricably bound to how fully a person lived the values and culture.

Shifting culture

Project Enterprise ran in full gear from 2006 to 2008. Leaders went through the workshops in batches: groups participated and returned, then the next group would go. Those not yet involved started to ask when their turn would come. While we had some early adopters – leaders who saw the benefits quickly and sent their whole business units through the training – others were slower to embrace change, and the programme initially met with some reluctance and cynicism.

Reluctance came through primarily in the form of complaints that we were spending too much money and time on this 'culture change thing'. I felt that this reluctance largely reflected people's discomfort, which in a way signalled that we were making inroads and touching the right nerves. Sasol's historical culture had not been the kind where you sat around talking about how you felt or about your colleagues' behaviour or what your value systems were. However, because the CEO and ExCo were driving the process, holding their own monthly workshops where they were beginning to talk about soft 'heart' issues, that reluctance was short-lived. Once the senior ExCo had these conversations with their own ExCos, the rest of the organisation realised this programme was here to stay and they might as well get on board.

The cynicism manifested around people questioning the programme's ability to bring lasting and real change. You'd hear sarcastic comments like: 'I saw somebody behaving in a way that was not values driven: they stole my parking space. What are you going to do about it?' Again, I mostly viewed such flippant comments as a good sign, to the extent that they showed that people were adopting the common language we had introduced in the workshops. Even if a person was not adopting the spirit behind the statement, the fact that the language was starting to seep into the culture was progress.

We also instituted financial incentives and sanctions. Although a developmental approach works better than a punitive one when it comes to buy-in, peer pressure and pride are quite effective motivators, and we needed to ensure that we weren't just talking about these things. In 2007 we ran a second Barrett culture perception survey so managers could see where their teams had made culture shifts and where they were still struggling. To incentivise everyone, we linked the adoption of the new culture and values to people's performance evaluations and their personal bottom line – about 10% of a senior leader's annual bonus (and 5% of a team member's) was linked to how well that person lived the values and drove and supported diversity within his or her team. Using the results of the Barrett Survey and employee engagement reports, we would be able to establish how the leader and their team were perceived by their peers, customers and employees with regard to living the values.

⋄⋄⋄⋄⋄

In spite of all these efforts, the process of change felt frustratingly slow to me, in part because we had set such high expectations across the organisation – for myself, for the leaders, and among all our black colleagues, many of whom were questioning why the change was taking so long. So even while behind the scenes I was working furiously, we also were receiving letters from disgruntled black employees saying that the organisation was not changing as fast as it should, and that the system was still riddled with numerous challenges that made it difficult for them to succeed. In response to this, in 2006 we established the Sasol Black Professionals Forum. Created to help the organisation continually engage with these issues, the forum helped keep us honest about our progress; because one thing that always remained very clear was that this process had to be nurtured on a daily basis.

Additionally, in 2007 we held a Diversity Indaba, where Sasol's top leadership came together to review what people were saying internally about the transformation process, and why black employees were still failing to be recognised and/or experiencing the company negatively. Some examples of issues that came out of the indaba were that certain businesses were still using Afrikaans as the language of communication in meetings, which frustrated employees who didn't speak it, and was also inappropriate for an international organisation.

In those first few years I was keenly aware that if we did not drive the process relentlessly, it ran the risk of not getting the traction needed to make the deeper change required. In taking this job on, I had raised expectations externally that Sasol was committed to transformation. I saw the agenda as so much bigger than Sasol though, and there was a lot at stake for me personally. On the one hand, I knew my BMF colleagues were keenly awaiting news of my success as their former president in changing this corporate behemoth; on the other, I knew Pat had made public commitments about transformation to all our stakeholders. We had so many eyes on us, and the consequences of failing in this grand project were unbearable to even consider.

In fact, my first twelve months at Sasol were so stressful that in December 2006 I landed in the Cardiac ICU at Morningside Clinic. Thankfully it turned out to be an aggravated anxiety attack rather than a heart attack, but the incident sobered me up and taught me to stop sweating the small stuff so much. I also had to learn the art of eating an elephant bit by bit to prevent indigestion, which in part meant allowing myself to rely on other people to drive the process along with me.

Pat Davies was an amazing support to me during this period. Publicly and privately, he never ceased to compliment my work and 'courage' in taking on Sasol's transformation. He always mentioned my 'famous' cold hands-warm heart speech, in which I had encouraged all of us to connect our hearts to our hands in order to get a change going in terms of how we managed people as an organisation.

In that same speech I had also pointed out that 'we were all racists, albeit Pavlovian ones at best'. By this I was referring to the ways our socialisation determined personal prejudices, and how our perceptions of the racial and gender divide were so often pre-determined and so subconscious that many people were shocked by their own 'latent instincts' when specific circumstances or situations caused them to surface. In other words, self-awareness was key for all of us in this journey.

By the time we had our annual Leadership Forum in 2007, we wanted to get as many of our leaders as possible to reflect on their own personal prejudices and the ways in which these influenced their perceptions and judgements of others. An opportunity presented itself with the recent release of the movie *Catch a Fire*. Based on the true story of Patrick Chamusso, one of our ex-employees from Sasol Secunda, the movie depicts how Mr Chamusso was framed and falsely accused of terrorism by the apartheid government. Responding to that injustice by joining Umkhonto we Sizwe, the militant arm of the ANC, Mr Chamusso later attempted an actual attack on our Secunda plant. For this, he was arrested and sentenced to 24 years on Robben Island. Released after ten years in the general amnesty of 1994, he was now living in Mpumalanga, not far from the Secunda plant. I persuaded Pat that it would be a great gesture towards 'reconciliation' to invite Mr Chamusso to address our Leadership Forum.

Mr Chamusso, who with his wife now ran a day-care centre for AIDS orphans, shared his message of reconciliation with our top 1 500 leaders. He knew that some of the people who had 'framed' him could be sitting in that audience, as the majority had been adults at the time of his arrest, and some would have been in service with Sasol back then. His talk on forgiveness was incredibly moving. It caused many in the audience to become emotionally overwhelmed. When he finished, dozens of people came to thank him for sharing his story, offering support for his centre, clearly moved to a real moment of soul searching.

The point here is twofold: first, apartheid had done its best to desensitise us to the human condition, and putting a face to one of the old regime's so-called terrorists – in this case, Patrick Chamusso – was important for those still around to acknowledge those past injustices and their own complicity in them. And second, almost everyone is looking for a way to reconnect at a human level, even if just symbolically, and sometimes all it takes to break through that desensitisation and recognise our common humanity is a willingness to listen to one another with empathy. We tried various ways to embark on personal soul-searching journeys as an organisation.

A higher purpose

Over time we started to see the desired shifts, some green shoots. Stakeholders began to comment positively about the culture transformation taking place, and the government began engaging with us in amazing ways, to the extent that Pat and the company were invited to join presidential delegations abroad on business (this was from the same President Mbeki who had published a letter criticising the company just a few years prior). I truly believe that a huge part of Sasol's successful culture change was due to having a CEO who was so visibly and personally committed to our massive organisational transformation, both internally and externally.

On reflection, I believe Pat was quite a rebel and also visionary. When talking about driving culture change, he liked to invoke a 'higher purpose', convinced that the real impact of our work went far beyond our profits. He believed that corporations had civic responsibilities in addition to paying taxes, and that we needed to engage with communities everywhere we worked. His notion of a 'higher purpose' and seeking meaning in what we did as a company resonated with many people in the organisation at a personal level.

Pat's high level of consciousness came from a willingness to examine personal behaviours and attitudes, and the self-awareness that allows you to see your own strengths and weaknesses, not just technically, but emotionally and socially in terms of how you engage as a person. There is a lot of introspection and growth that you need to either have done or be ready to do. This is key. Once you as a leader start talking about values and culture – effectively becoming a custodian of this process in an organisation – you put your own life under the spotlight, and therefore need to be living more consciously yourself. The ability to bring that authenticity and vulnerability to the table is extremely important, but it only comes from having embarked on your own transformation journey at a personal level.

As mentioned, the transformation journey never ends, and as leaders we often coached each other as we moved through the different stages. I remember an incident that occurred after I had been at Sasol for about six months. I had started to notice that after Pat would ask me to do something, he would often ask another colleague to do the same thing. I brought this up with him, asking why he was doing it, as it felt like he was second-guessing me.

'I'm actually trying to help,' he said. 'The organisation is still new for you, and it is so big. These people know the organisation better.'

'Okay, but out there it appears as if you don't trust that I will deliver. It doesn't send a good message. Even if it's not intentional, it will have negative and unintended consequences on the organisation,' I explained.

'I'm sorry, you're right,' he agreed. 'In our next ExCo session I'd like you to raise this again. But do it the way you just have with me so we can have this conversation and role model to the team how a person can do things with unintended consequences, and also how a conversation like this can take place without being dysfunctional or negative.'

We did just that at our next monthly ExCo session. There was a facilitator present for those sessions, and when we replayed the conversation within the ExCo team, you could see how it caused others to reflect on how often they did things – often a result of being under time pressure or thinking they were helping someone – that had unintended negative consequences.

Another realisation that came out of this discussion was the importance of context. If Pat had done the same thing to a young white man, his actual intention – to mentor and support a new employee still learning the ropes – would have come through positively. But by doing it to me – the first female and black person at my level – it communicated a lack of trust or a sense that I could not cope on my own. In other words, the narrative is never going to be the same for a black woman and a white man, even if your intention is pure and honest.

In addition to these learnings around unintended consequences of actions, there was a big lesson about the importance of a leader's willingness to make himself vulnerable. For Pat as CEO to make himself that vulnerable – with me, in front of the team, and in general – was so significant to our ability to change the culture in the organisation. What that vulnerability gained us was trust: when a leader is prepared to show vulnerability, people are much more likely to engage constructively and openly themselves, and this is invaluable.

CHAPTER 12

◇◇◇◇◇◇◇◇◇◇◇◇◇◇◇◇

Thinking globally, acting locally

Operating in 35 countries and carrying a secondary listing on the New York Stock Exchange, Sasol was a global player in all respects. In a refreshing role reversal from the norm in those days, our global offices looked to South Africa for policy. If we needed to develop or change an HR policy, it could not be done in Germany or China, but rather had to come through our head office in Rosebank. As executive director of Strategy and HR, I owned every HR policy, and as the third most senior person in the organisation (after the CEO and CFO), my responsibilities and perspectives both in terms of our business possibilities and the larger transformation agenda grew tremendously.

It was fascinating for me to see how the South African perspective on transformation was valued globally because of the complexity of our society, given its transition since 1994. International business people were extremely curious to know more about how South African businesses approached and negotiated their BEE, employment equity and skills development responsibilities.

The South African perspective always adds value to any conversation about transformation. Due to the transformation laws that are unique to our business environment, South African leaders and managers must deal with more complexities than their counterparts in Europe or even the United

States, especially when it comes to our legislative framework around labour issues and our transitioning culture.

My international exposure with Sasol also demonstrated the degree to which our isolation as a country pre-1994 had affected our perceptions of the rest of the world. On the one hand, South Africans are afflicted with a global inferiority complex, believing the best and greatest to always be somewhere else 'out there', while on the other we tend to greatly underestimate our counterparts on the African continent. Although when it comes to benchmarking you often do still need to look abroad, it is equally true that South African business also demonstrates some of the best and greatest in terms of our processes, especially when it comes to community engagement, small and medium enterprise development, and diversity and inclusion.

Meanwhile, I continue to find it curious that while our national inferiority complex is based in the belief that people beyond our borders do everything better, we wrongly continue to imagine that our counterparts on the continent do things worse. Whether on holiday, in a business meeting, or even at the government level, it embarrasses me to say that I have all too often seen South Africans relating to fellow Africans with this delusional sense of superiority. I say delusional because generally speaking, I have found our African counterparts smarter and sharper in their business suss and acumen than the average South African. I suspect it is partly because our African colleagues tend to seek more international exposure than we do, are more resilient emotionally, and thus frequently possess a worldlier perspective than someone who has only operated in the South African space.

⧖⧖⧖

My own global exposure was growing apace. As executive director of Strategy and HR, my portfolio was extended to include Risk, Safety, Health and Environment, and Corporate Affairs – cross-cutting organisational functions that required my direct involvement in a range of policies that influenced and affected entire regions. For instance, I worked with our American team in Louisiana to develop a customised corporate affairs policy for Sasol's operations in the USA, partnering with the Louisiana Economic Development Center to improve inclusion of small minority-owned businesses from the local community by applying tools from our South African BEE framework.

Such international exposure provided new vantages on the nuances of culture change and the importance of context to any programme of change. Operating in so many different environments, we had to be alive to the local factors affecting diversity, while still ensuring that our fundamental values and way of doing things didn't change significantly simply because we found ourselves in an environment with different challenges. In other words, when designing any global programme, it was vital that it be founded in a well-considered philosophy in keeping with Sasol's core values, but remained easily adaptable to local regional issues, and was not overly prescriptive.

For example, we encouraged female employees in every country of operation to establish a Women's Business Forum (WBF) to support gender equity in the workplace. While in Qatar the agenda was around getting involved in mentorship projects and supporting other organisations or charitable groups in the community, the German WBF focused on questions of how to retain professional women. Meanwhile the South African WBF was equally concerned with career progression and the mentorship of younger women. This all made sense given that in Qatar 90% of the women in the forum were still at junior management levels, whereas in South Africa you had women across the spectrum and levels, and in Germany, external government incentives for women to raise families encouraged them to take time out. In other words, the needs of women in business differed from region to region, but our overall philosophy, which was to support those needs, held firm across the board.

I also enjoyed learning about the similarities and differences in terms of how countries dealt with their different affirmative action efforts. In Qatar, a country whose history and culture couldn't be more different than ours in South Africa, they talked about 'Qatarization', a government scheme that granted employment preference to Qatari citizens and required that all Qatari citizens received a minimum salary increase – something that would have been impossible to manage in another jurisdiction. Meanwhile the Mozambican government's 'localisation programme' required multinational companies operating in Mozambique to submit a plan outlining skills development programmes, number of locals in management positions and a process to ensure that a certain percentage of Mozambicans would eventually be involved in running operations over time.

Like South Africa's BEE, all of those interventions were concerned with economic empowerment for indigenous populations, although each country called it something else. Having our own clear transformation policy at Sasol was essential when navigating between local regulations in different countries. As we interpreted policies from one country to another, we always brought it back to the need to ensure consistency and harmony with our overall group policy.

That process of finding consistency and harmony while interrogating the 'case studies' represented by different countries and contexts tremendously broadened and deepened my understanding of how we could enhance our own transformation efforts in South Africa. For example, the 'diversity and inclusion' concept, which is about the qualitative process that merges issues of culture change, values and creating an environment where employees with different diversity dimensions can thrive, was broadly used internationally, especially in the USA at that time. By contrast, although the South African conversation certainly acknowledged 'inclusion' issues, we were far more focused on the numbers and targets around ownership and employment equity.

Seeing what was happening around culture change globally strengthened my already held conviction that we needed to keep pulling the qualitative issues (the diversity and inclusion aspects) together with the quantitative issues (the ownership and employment targets) in order to make real change. In design, the BEE Act and Employment Equity Act were not intended to look exclusively at targets, but also to make provisions around recruitment, skills development, culture and, to a certain extent, salary equity (the income differentials). By truly merging these two concepts in practice, we could achieve so much more than the legislation has achieved.

It was with this spirit that we drove Sasol's transformation. In other words, we believed the numbers mattered, but so did the culture and environment. In fact, the two work together: without a critical mass of diverse people within your workforce, you will not create a worthwhile environment, and without a transformed environment, the 'diversity' you bring cannot thrive as it should. A final note on the 'critical mass': one or two people will not make a change. You need a critical mass of diverse people in key visible positions because this is how you create role models who ensure that the system continues to evolve and grow.

Milestones

The change I so fiercely wanted to see started to show signs of taking hold in my third year at Sasol. More black professionals held very senior positions, and by 2008 about 20% of our top 100 people (from 0 to 20) were black, including three (from 0 to 3) black managing directors (in mining, oil and gas).

In 2007 we established the Sasol Women's Forum, which created a space where gender issues were openly discussed among our top female leaders. Pat championed the forum, hosting the sessions and personally inviting our female leaders to attend, largely because of many women's initial reluctance to be associated with a 'women's thing'. The irony of needing a senior-level male to give legitimacy to this forum was not lost on us, but this is how things go – it was the same when we started the Black Professionals Forum: without such 'endorsement', people would have been concerned that their managers might view their involvement with suspicion.

This reluctance speaks to the importance of institutionalising such groups, an act that validates people's participation and gives them permission to discuss their issues as a group. Individuals who were familiar with the BMF's corporate activist environment were more comfortable talking about these issues transparently, which was helpful for those who initially struggled with the idea of being identified as part of a 'special interest group' (as the Americans would say).

But the openness that these forums soon enjoyed reflected and reinforced the directional shift taking place in the overall culture. That shift could be heard in the conversations people were having and even the way people spoke, with the values-driven language becoming increasingly commonplace from tea rooms to boardrooms. Additionally, in 2007 we finally had our first black female chairman of the board in Hixonia Nyasulu.

Another 'face' of Sasol's paradigm shift, Hixonia was originally invited to join the board in 2006, and her influence as chairman was a key part of our transformation. Having come to Sasol from Unilever, a PLC global company, her perspectives and ability to speak comfortably about issues of diversity and inclusion across race, gender, religion and all the other dimensions of diversity helped change paradigms within Sasol's board. Hixonia was and still is the most humble yet profoundly intelligent woman I know in business. Being in such close quarters with a business leader of her stature was inspirational for me, particularly as I had never before had a visible black female role model within a company where I worked. Seeing how she handled her powerful position with such competence and elegance, while always making herself accessible to other women and young people, both inside the company and externally, was simply wonderful.

◇◇◇◇◇

In 2008 Sasol pulled off the largest BEE transaction in South Africa. Valued at R26 billion, Sasol's Inzalo BEE Transaction fulfilled our BEE target of 10% black ownership of the company. I ran the Inzalo project with a team of about 40 people. Through a public participation process, we informed the public of the details, which came down to shares being made available at a 12–13% reduction, with a minimum purchase of 25 shares. With the prospectus available at the post office, people simply indicated how many shares they wanted, and then 30 days later they found out how many shares they had secured. Masses of people lined up to buy the shares, and Inzalo ended up nearly five times over-subscribed, resulting in applicants receiving only 25% of the shares applied for. (Because of the over-subscription I withdrew my own application, purchasing my shares two months later at market value.)

Inzalo was a huge success, not only because of its total value, but more importantly because the shares did not just go to a handful of the 'usual suspects'. Because Inzalo was open to the general public, Sasol ended up with over 200 000 black shareholders. For Inzalos' ten-year span (in the first three years you could sell shares only to other black people, after ten years you could sell on the open market), we continually engaged those shareholders, mainly through our AGMs. Those AGMs were their own story, as they served as an opportunity to educate black South Africans about the economy, and what it meant to own shares in a company. Because of the number of shareholders, we held multiple AGMs every year. With about 3 000 shareholders per gathering, we translated the proceedings into six South African languages so everyone understood what it meant to own shares and be part of this journey (as a result, our AGMs lasted for the whole day rather than the usual one to two hours). We also connected Inzalo to a foundation, through which some R800 million went into STEM education (for example, science workbooks, mobile science labs, and over 500 bursaries for tertiary study).

The only unfortunate aspect of the transaction was that it happened right before the financial market crash of 2008/09. As a result, it took much longer for people to make something out of their shares, even with the initial discounted buying price. But from a process perspective, it remains one of the country's hallmark BEE transactions in that it achieved full inclusive participation. This was particularly important in light of our larger goal of repositioning Sasol in people's minds: we wanted black South Africans to feel ownership in the company, and through Inzalo we enabled thousands, literally, to own a stake. Over the years we have regularly received letters of thanks, especially from employees – from secretaries to people in our factories – each time they receive another dividend.

◇◇◇◇◇

Another first for us at that time was the creation of the Sasol Partnership Forum, a platform where management and all five of our unions could meet to discuss key strategic transformation issues. Until then, management-labour conversations normally focused on salaries and wages to the exclusion of all else. The forum was therefore created to establish a space of trust where Sasol employees could meet and discuss common agendas related to transformation both with one another as well as with management. It was a completely new concept, and when my Employee Relations manager, Mxolisi Raitsibe, proposed it, I initially thought it sounded crazy.

'I think it will work,' he insisted. 'We've already done a lot of the work around culture change and our values-driven process. I think the unions are ready for it and will be interested if we propose it.'

For nearly a year an external facilitator led detailed consultations with the unions to agree on protocols for working together, definitions for the platform's values and culture, and finally to establish the formal terms of reference.

Mxolisi was proven right. The forum was truly transformational as a platform, bringing together our different unions, which spanned the ideological spectrum from the mainly white and far right Solidarity Union, to the COSATU-affiliated CEPPAWU and NUM. All five of our unions embraced the platform, which gave them a common space to discuss issues of mutual concern, like safety, learning and development, and overall employee wellness. The forum helped stabilise labour relations in the company, and is a model now used by most companies with multiple unions.

◇◇◇◇◇

It was also in my third year with Sasol that the opportunity arose to shift our sports sponsorship to align with our transformation agenda. For years Sasol had sponsored men's rugby through the Springboks. When that contract came to an end in 2008, I suggested that we use our sponsorship to focus explicitly on transformation, nation-building and teamwork, while also choosing a team that our support could develop and connect to the company's ethos of high performance.

I discussed the matter with my corporate affairs team, and we looked at various sports codes but struggled to find the right match. One weekend when I was home channel-hopping, I paused on something that looked like an international awards ceremony, partially translated from French. I was only half paying attention, but as these athletic women kept coming onstage – some in ballgowns – my attention focused. Eventually the presenter said, 'Once again welcome back to FIFA Sports Women' awareness'. I had never even realised women's football existed (I must admit that I am not a very sporty person). In any case, I did some googling, and later that evening sent an SMS to one of my corporate affairs team members, asking her to please follow up on FIFA Women.

On Monday Andriesa Singleton, head of sports marketing within the corporate affairs team, stopped by my office, clearly very excited.

'You know, we [the corporate affairs team] had been wanting to support Banyana Banyana, but people said it wasn't a good idea,' she said, referring to South Africa's women's football team.

'It's brilliant, Let's go for it!' I said, thrilled at the prospect. Which is how Sasol became the sole sponsor of Banyana Banyana.

When we first came along, the women's sports kit consisted of the leftovers from Bafana Bafana (the men's team) and they had no games scheduled. Our support enabled them to acquire quality female kit, and they quickly went from being unrated on the continent to playing twice in the Olympics. One of my proudest moments remains the day Banyana Banyana qualified for their first match at the 2012 London Olympics five years later.

Sasol also went on to sponsor South Africa's national wheelchair basketball team, which went to the Olympics as well. Banyana Banyana and the wheelchair basketball team both made Sasol and South Africa proud over and over, and our choice to sponsor them embodied the company's paradigm shift and new mindset, which affirmed that diversity and excellence go together.

⋄⋄⋄⋄⋄

A final, and by many estimations most significant, milestone came in 2009, when Sasol's business operations started noting clear connections between teams that were strongly values driven and operationally excellent in terms of performance.

The data that we used for our incentives (the 5–10% of people's annual bonuses) came from assessments evaluating how well a team or individual was doing in terms of living and driving the culture and values – information largely gleaned from the Barrett Survey that we continued to run annually. Because the Barrett Survey was a 360-degree evaluation, it reflected not only what your people said and did, but also how your peers viewed your team or organisation.

Across the company, people started noticing and recognising the link between teams that scored well on the Barrett Survey, those that enjoyed more cohesive team relationships, and those whose performance was improving. It came down to the fact that teams that communicate better tend to share information better, have fewer safety incidents, and are more productive and operationally excellent.

This is not rocket science, and there really were not too many surprises when you saw the Barrett results and knew the teams. None the less, engineers and scientists tended to particularly value this kind of 'hard' correlation, so these results gave our culture change programme the momentum it needed to achieve mainstream acceptance. By 2010 the only people who stuck out were those not driving the process.

Personal success

One of the greatest aspects of my life in Joburg as a single professional woman was the strong friendships I was able to develop with other professional women whose careers span the legal, business and political fields. Almost immediately upon relocating to Joburg for good, I realised I had numerous female peers and mentors to call on both professionally and socially. I was invited by some of these friends to join a 'stokvel'. Traditionally a savings or investment society in which members regularly contribute an agreed amount, from which they each get a turn receiving a lump sum payment, our group of ladies turned out to be more concerned with letting our hair down than we were with raising money. We were all in high-profile executive jobs and needed a 'safe' space in which to exhale.

About fifteen to 20 of us met monthly at someone's house, generally with our kids in tow. Typically, at the end of the evening, signalling that it was time to depart for home, the host would play the beautiful *Waiting to Exhale* soundtrack, and we would all heartily sing along to 'Count on Me', cementing our commitment to emotionally support each other from month to month. Over the course of these monthly gatherings and regular holidays spent together, these women and their families became Phila's and my extended family. With our children becoming friends and gaining an extended network of aunties, this social and familial anchor of women has kept me going for almost 20 years now.

CHAPTER 13

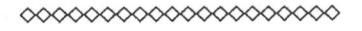

Extending my reach

When I joined Sasol I had specifically been brought in because of my experience in HR, strategy and culture change processes. However, for some time I had aspired to get more experience around operations. In my initial negotiations with Pat, we had agreed that in addition to leading the processes so urgently required by the company around culture change, my work would over time be integrated into multiple aspects of the business, including more exposure to operations.

The allure of operations was twofold: first, it is widely considered the heart of any business, and second, it remained an area rarely populated by women or black people. So naturally it was a tantalising challenge and a box I wanted to tick. I believe a large part of why so few women or black people make it to operations comes down to trust – that is, leaders trusting you to handle such a key 'stretch' opportunity delivering on the 'core' business. Stretch opportunities are naturally perceived to carry a certain risk, and so the question of *how* you select someone for such a chance is paramount. After all, if you cannot objectively demonstrate a successful track record of delivering '1 000 nuts and bolts', what other objective measurements can the organisation use to say that you are the right person to get the job done when the opportunity arises? This is where the unquantifiable quality of trust comes in.

I have found that earning trust is as much about making people feel comfortable and confident that you know what you are doing as it is about proving technical competence. And the reality is that people tend to be more comfortable with – and therefore trusting of – people who look and sound like them. This truth has translated historically to white male leaders having more trust for other white males. In reverse, this subjective 'instinct' translates as a lack of confidence in or comfort around someone who looks and sounds different, meaning that if you do not know that person and so have no track record of working together, there is an absence of 'trust', even though that person may have all the required competencies. The consequence of this subconscious trust (or its absence) is far-reaching and profound, influencing people's perceptions of others and manifesting in appointments being made on a subjective basis.

Fortunately, such perception issues can be dealt with if senior leadership is willing to engage in honest and open conversations about how to integrate transformation and diversity into talent management and succession planning processes. These can be difficult conversations, forcing people to examine why they might think that a black or female candidate does not appear to have the capacity or capability to be the next key person in the organisation and, if that is their perception, what are they doing as management to rectify that? In other words, how is management proactively developing junior staff so that in three to five years they are equally capable of taking on a 'stretch' opportunity?

It is only when we create and use unbiased systems – which must include some measure for culture – that we can talk about fully equal access to opportunity, which is so fundamental to real transformation. This was something we talked about a lot at the BMF, as many people mistakenly believe that equal access to opportunity is simply a question of advertising a job that is 'open' to 'everyone' to apply. Because of the great inequality that we come from in South Africa, truly equalising opportunity required – and still requires – active effort from everyone to change the culture in our institutions, especially in business.

As leaders it is up to us to create the environment that enables people to grow to their full potential, and a huge part of this is about having the right enabling culture in place. In the case of private sector senior leadership, this means ensuring that performance management systems can consistently and fairly measure performance, ability and potential. This does not require a radical rethink of performance management systems, as most systems function well in terms of measuring those things. The failure of these systems comes primarily from *not* measuring the culture (that is, how enabling is the culture for all individuals to prosper and grow in the company, and how well is the person delivering in terms of promoting that culture?), as well as from the potential subjectivity of the assessor.

Ninety per cent of performance management systems will function fairly and consistently if you add culture as one of the measures that a person is expected to deliver on. If you have defined the desired values, culture and behaviours upfront, you can consistently measure everyone against these. Obviously, you'll have a problem if the values and behaviour are not clearly defined, as the system requires that everyone uses the same definitions to function properly. In other words, you must already have done the work of co-defining the values and sharing them across the organisation before you can incorporate them into an employee assessment system. But once this has happened, you have created the necessary context to measure or assess performance when it comes to living the defined values and culture.

This type of performance management system, which takes culture and values into account, enables diverse candidates to compete successfully for stretch opportunities and usually does away with choices made due to 'subconscious trust' or its absence. Once culture and values are integrated into the talent management and succession planning processes, you can look at someone who is a great performer – technically *and* culturally – and focus on asking what management is doing to move that person to the next level or opportunity. Whether this means a business unit rotation or stint on an academic or short course, these are the kinds of personal development conversations that lead to a person growing in new areas like management and/or hard operations. This is key, as there comes a point in a person's career when it is difficult to rotate into a top position if you have not been exposed to certain development experiences early enough, as these skills do not materialise overnight.

Getting noticed

As head of HR, another process I was concerned with was how junior people got noticed by top leadership (and therefore were offered development opportunities), and how to ensure maximum transparency of this process. As with performance management systems, the issue of getting noticed comes down to organisations asking who they are mentoring and selecting for development opportunities and on what basis.

In addition to the more formal structures of assessments and rotations, there are additional informal ways for junior employees to stand out, yet there is no handbook advertising these processes. While I was at Sasol I chaired numerous group committees over the years. Although every committee included members whose role and function required their participation, most committees also included people over and above those members. Committees therefore represent a development platform for the next layer of management to show the depth and breadth of its talent to senior management. These kinds of committee presentations can be great exposure for a rising star, and therefore should be seen as a skills development opportunity.

For example, if the head of Safety is presenting a paper to the committee, this is an opportunity for one or two others who have worked on the team preparing that paper to participate and shine. Even just sitting in on a committee session serves a purpose for a junior person. I always advise managers to use committee presentations to give exposure to their high-potential people. Such presentations offer a safe place to give people you are developing an opportunity to field questions, which is an important part of growth. That said, if one of your people ends up ill prepared or can't engage at the level expected, you as their line manager need to be ready to step in and protect your team; letting a junior member hang is not a good reflection on you or your team.

Junior people often imagine that mentorship relationships come about when some senior person 'notices' you and decides to take you under her wing, but the reality is that more often than not it's up to you to get yourself noticed. Thus, young professionals with ambition should volunteer to be on committees: ask to join and then make yourself useful in whatever way possible, even if it just means taking notes. The point is to get in the room, and once you are there, get as much exposure as you can. Never look at any work that needs to be done as 'beneath' you. You may spend six months taking notes before the opportunity you seek appears, but it is this kind of commitment that managers and leaders are looking for, as everyone knows you are doing the work over and above your actual job. Building a reputation as someone who is always willing to lend additional hands and feet and brains, you will find people calling you the next time an opportunity arises.

When I started my career the only way to get in the room was offering to be the secretary to take notes, which included making tea. Irritating as this may have been, while I was making the tea I was listening to the discussions and getting important exposure to what was happening 'behind closed doors'. Particularly because in many organisations senior people seem inaccessible, there is great value in demystifying what it is they sit around doing all day. Although I did not relish participating in the gender stereotype of a black woman making the tea, I knew my goal, and so was able to see my tea duty as part of a larger plan.

Even today, if I am in a meeting and no one is taking notes, I will sometimes volunteer. After all, I am taking my own notes anyway, and so by offering to take and share the minutes, the process of clarifying what is in my notes gives me an opportunity to engage more deeply with whoever is leading the session. The point is, these sorts of 'extra' actions telegraph your interest and provide opportunities for greater discussion. Do not equate taking notes with keeping quiet or being subservient.

Ultimately it all comes down to knowing what you are looking for so that when an opportunity comes you don't miss it simply because it is not labelled or defined in the expected form. This relates to a larger point about career moves. Sometimes you make a career move that won't make sense from other people's perspectives. As in the game of chess, your strategy often will include a sideways or even backwards move to get you in the right position to succeed. What matters is knowing that each move is taking you closer to your final aspiration.

Change and evolution

In June 2010 Pat Davies retired after six years as CEO and 37 years as a Sasol employee, and David Constable stepped in as our new CEO. Coming from his position as VP at Fluor, David was an engineer with 30 years of global engineering, procurement and construction (EPC) experience, and was well suited to guide Sasol to deliver its next stage of projects, which would call on those EPC skills.

Relocating from his native Canada, David's outsider perspective provided some interesting impressions concerning our culture issues and progress with diversity and inclusion. For example, he was taken aback by the continued use of Afrikaans in some parts of the organisation. This observation sensitised employees from all backgrounds to the ways in which language can be problematic when it comes to inclusion. With a majority of black South Africans speaking to one another in African languages, we had to acknowledge that people who don't understand those languages also end up feeling excluded. Although Xhosa, Zulu and Sotho do not carry the same associative baggage as Afrikaans – which historically served as a language of exclusion and was the dominant language in businesses under apartheid – exclusion is still exclusion. In a country with twelve official languages (if we include sign language), the question of finding a balance between not always speaking a home language while still promoting inclusive culture remains unresolved.

Overall, however, David was impressed by our approach to transformation. I still remember one of our first conversations when I approached our new CEO to clearly state my expectations of him as our top leader.

'Pat and I had an understanding that he would work with me to champion and visibly lead the transformation agenda,' I said. I knew that establishing terms with my boss was unorthodox, but after five years running culture change, I was all too aware that I could not do my job properly without his explicit support. 'You have been chosen by the board, and I am excited to work together, but I need you to know my expectations of you as our leader in this area,' I continued.

David was clearly surprised by this, but to his credit he heard me out. That said, I think it took him a few months to understand my ongoing sense of urgency around culture change. I did not want us to lose the momentum we had built as an organisation around our values.

'It's working, nothing is broken, why are you going on about it?' he would say.

'You have to own it. It's not my process. It is mine from a function perspective, but it's yours to lead,' I would insist in return.

It took us a while to get to the point of finding each other, but we got there. After David met with the unions through the Sasol Partnership Forum, as well as the Sasol Black Professional Forum, he understood why the issues remained urgent. In his third month as CEO, sporting a pink tie, David proudly gave the keynote address to about 1 000 Sasol women attending our Women's Month celebration event. Later that afternoon we all carried on to Orlando Stadium in Soweto to watch Banyana Banyana play and win one of their first Olympics pre-qualifying soccer matches. I was beyond excited. We had found our new transformation champion in David.

False dichotomies

Like all new CEOs, David did a 'cabinet reshuffle', reviewing and tweaking the top team to best suit his vision and strategy for the company's future. Handing Strategy to David as CEO, I remained executive director of HR, where Sasol's values and culture change programme was anchored. Additionally I took on

Corporate Affairs, Risk, Safety, and Health and Environment. I was happy because my new diversified portfolio brought me much closer to operations and with these changes I also became executive vice president.

As mentioned, I had been keen to work more closely with operations for quite some time, and over the years I had got involved with all of Sasol's different business units in various ways. First, as the head of Group Strategy and HR, I had been involved in each business unit's individual strategy as well as its global HR issues. Second, like all executive directors and group ExCo members, I served as a director on the boards of about six different business units, including Sasol Mining.

Early in 2010 I became the chairman of Sasol Mining's board. As a business of scale whose growth was important to the company, mining was one of the country's key transformation areas and therefore of particular interest to me. As chairman, I sat in on weekly operations meetings and worked closely with the mining executive Riaan Rademan, a passionate miner who had worked in the sector for over 25 years. Riaan taught me that running a successful mining business was as much about understanding people as it was about the technical mining processes. That is, the ability to create a productive environment relied on clear and positive communications with your workforce.

As I worked with the business teams in my new portfolio areas of Risk, Safety, and Health and Environment, what became increasingly clear to me was that positive and clear communication was at the heart of everything. From having a great record – be it in safety, health or the environment to general risk management – Sasol's successful operations relied on a healthy organisational culture as much as they did on our people's technical competence.

The closer I got to operations, the more I realised it was in many ways a continuation of the work I had been doing, integrating the values and culture and behaviour changes into the organisation so that these qualities could continue to underpin operational excellence. Something I had long suspected was confirmed: that culture, people and values are the heart of every successful business.

Although I did not carry line responsibility for the profit and loss of the business units I headed, the exposure I got to operations through my new portfolio satisfied the need I once had to tick that box. Earlier in my career I had seen how working in operations accelerated people's career trajectories and had wished to be more directly involved in ops. But having got to the top of the organisation without that experience, and now being involved at the group level in the operations of a massive global manufacturing and energy company, I realised I had scratched this itch and then some. As Pat and David both put it, 'It can't get better than this portfolio. What else would you want to do that you haven't done?'

◇◇◇◇◇

On reflection, I think part of my desire to get into operations had been to see the view from the other side of the fence that seemingly separated 'hard' and 'soft' business issues. When you'd say, 'We've run 800 workshops on culture change' or 'We've touched the lives of 5 000 leaders in the organisation', it sounded great, but someone always pointed to the bottom line, asking, 'Yes, but did we sell more or fewer nuts and bolts?' I understood the tangible appeal of operations: if someone says she's produced 1 000 nuts and bolts, there is no arguing with that. You either produced 1 000, or fewer, or more. However, what I came to learn from working in operations was that the 'hard/soft' dichotomy was a false distinction.

Reflecting on the challenges we faced in functions, where your job is figuring out *how* the company will produce those 1 000 nuts and bolts – ensuring that all the necessary supporting machinery is running smoothly and the right people show up every day and are willing to work together – I realised with complete clarity that operations and functions are two sides of the same coin: without the one, the other may as well not exist. As much as I understood the desire to measure success or impact in quantifiable terms, the perspective I had gained from operations gave me an even deeper appreciation for the unquantifiable yet very real value of 'the how'.

This is where culture's impact on performance – a topic I find endlessly fascinating – comes in. One of the ultimate goals in organisational transformation is to integrate culture change and performance to the point where people recognise that it is *because of* your change to culture – and how it has affected the way you do things, including engaging with customers and stakeholders – that you now sell more nuts and bolts than you would have done had you continued doing things the old way. That has been the journey over the years, and that is also part of why I wanted direct involvement in operations, so I could experience things from the performance side.

But the barrier separating 'hard' and 'soft' business elements is actually disappearing as future business sustainability is increasingly seen as dependent on the 'how' and the value that resides there. For example, at Sasol we were able to demonstrate that when engaging with government departments or communities for licensing or permitting, the end result often had more to do with questions of culture than it did with how meticulously you completed a form. I directly experienced instances where particular government inspectors came and somehow found everything wrong with our application. Examining the result, you'd see that the inspector had focused on seemingly petty issues that could have just as easily been bypassed or corrected. Digging deeper about how the conversation with the inspector had gone, you'd then find that our people had behaved poorly, perhaps with arrogance or a lack of respect. Someone called it the 'traffic police test': how politely taking responsibility (rather than impatiently denying your offence) is the best way to walk away with a friendly warning rather than a fine. In other words, underlying issues around attitude can thwart you, and that comes down to culture. Simply put, cultures of respect, courtesy and professionalism yield constructive conversations and greater productivity.

When I came to Sasol in 2005, I found a strong organisation that was performing and doing well. Thanks to our culture change, Sasol now performs even better. How do we know this? It would be disingenuous for me to point to increased revenue or growth figures, and claim they are all a direct result of our culture change. But while it is true that Sasol has grown, the most significant indicator of our success is that our employees are happier to be there. Our culture change at Sasol was not just about getting more black people or women in the organisation: it was about opening the organisation up to create a more respectful and humanising environment.

Examples such as our Partnership Forum, where management and unions can speak freely and openly, led to employees feeling their views were accepted and welcome. As a result, they made suggestions that helped improve productivity and prevented safety incidents across various business units. On a larger scale, labour unrest reduced across the organisation, saving weeks or even months of lost work days. At the heart of this kind of change were the values demonstrated by all employees, including management, and a behaviour change that gave employees a sense of belonging and ownership over what was taking place in the company.

In this way, culture change was also fundamental to changing attitudes towards safety and employee wellness. Putting safety first and talking about the culture of safety led to fewer safety incidents for the company, which again increased productivity. Employee wellness became not only about preventing harm in the workplace, but also about nurturing the sense among our employees that they were valued as contributors. That value in turn unlocks potential, causing team members to contribute more than they would in a culture that does not recognise them as innovators or voices deserving to be heard.

We know we have achieved these things because people aspire to work for our company. We see that our employee value proposition is high, because when we talk to graduates in the industry, they want to work for Sasol *because* our brand has a good reputation and our leaders are known to be visionary. Knowing that your leaders do things with a sense of a higher purpose, that your employees are good ambassadors because they experience your culture positively, and that your company is at the top of the best young graduates' wishlist: these are things by which a company's success must also be measured.

PART 4: GLOBAL TRANSFORMATIONS

The next challenge

In 2014 when, after five years as CEO, David advised the board that he would not renew his contract, I had to consider my own next move. By that point I could say we had delivered the culture change shift that had been required. Sasol had gone from being a business people were not relating to as a South African entity to one of the country's most admired companies. It went from being a place where 100% of its top leadership was white and male to one where over 30% of our top 100 leaders were women and/or black. The organisation had moved from having a white CEO to having a black CEO in Bongani Nqwababa (albeit joint CEO and president). Indeed, Sasol had become a truly great and committed corporate citizen and a role model in terms of demonstrating how a large organisation could embrace transformation in a growing economy.

At Sasol I had been given the opportunity to increase the scale, diversity and depth of what I could handle as a leader. I had also had the rare privilege of being surrounded by people with the best qualifications and experience that money could buy in industry, and had almost come to take for granted the tremendous resources at my disposal to be the best I could be. In that extraordinary space, I had honed a leadership style that was anchored in values, integrity and principles, and always considered the bigger picture. As a leader I fundamentally acknowledged that I often did not know everything about an issue, and thus always endeavoured to bring other people's perspectives on board – something that was facilitated by the fact that I had surrounded myself with brilliant and talented people who challenged me intellectually, at whatever level they operated in the organisation.

I considered my Sasol years the culmination of everything I had done and experienced until then. Professionally, socially and spiritually, every experience I had had since being a child in my mother's shop had come together here. In retrospect it felt like all those other experiences served as rehearsals for this big part in what had finally been the real show. However, after eleven years and all the changes we had made and the impact I believe I had, it was the logical time for me to take a bow.

A tribute by Imogen Mkhize

On the occasion of the Annual Chairman's Dinner on 23 November 2016, where the board and the executive management were bidding farewell to David Constable and myself, I was deeply touched by the words Imogen Mkhize, non-executive director of Sasol, had to say about my time there:

> When we think of authentic leadership – leadership not born out of a position of authority; when we consider practical leadership, which helps individuals and organisations adapt and thrive in challenging environments; leadership that resonates with meaningful and positive change; and indeed, leadership that is anchored in emotional intelligence, humility and genuine kindness – it is often hard to find all of these desirable traits in one individual. But here at Sasol we've had the privilege to witness this kind of leadership in action.
>
> Ladies and gentlemen, this evening we celebrate and honour Ms Nolitha Fakude. Without a doubt Ms Fakude has the character, the skill and courage of a truly authentic leader. With her genuine attention to people development, she has been a catalyst that has consistently mobilised and collaborated positive change in this organisation since her arrival in 2005 as the first woman executive director of Sasol in its entire history.
>
> When Nolitha came to Sasol, she already had a history of a successful career. Since her Black Management Forum days, her life was about the development of people and the meaningful transformation of organisation. It was a life filled with learnings and activities that enabled her to lead and inspire people.
>
> Over the last eleven years, Nolitha has been relentless in bringing the Sasol values to life. Her commitment in keeping the company's moral code at the forefront of everyone's mind has been evident in all our engagements with her. In general, Nolitha's whole orientation and natural inclination often remind us that the key values of safety, people, integrity and accountability are not only essential but they can shift a

PART 4: GLOBAL TRANSFORMATIONS

culture and make a sustainable difference.

Driven by respect, trust, collaboration and teamwork, Nolitha has been the force that has guided this organisation through some of the challenges and obstacles that were enormous, not least of which was the global financial crisis a mere three years into her tenure. She has been part of a few other transitions at Sasol – and I'm certain that some of them required her to move beyond her comfort zone, but she certainly measured up.

Among her colleagues, she has been the trusted adviser, a skilled executor, and she has helped transform this organisation not just from an empowerment point of view, but also from a business point of view.

I dare say, one of Nolitha's greatest attributes is that she does not often come from a place where she has all the answers, because when you do there's never an opportunity for anybody else to express themselves. Nolitha is blessed with that subtle perception to enquire and seek understanding which helps her mobilise and co-create without reaching conclusions on her own. People often respond very positively to that personality trait; it empowers and builds confidence in people. As we open ourselves for growth, we also enable those around us to grow.

Nolitha, your tireless efforts in your beliefs, your keen judgement and sheer humanism, the passion that you have to do what is right, have been an incredible asset to this organisation. Your indomitable commitment and purposeful work ethic has helped Sasol meet the challenges of a demanding era. As I was preparing these remarks, I spoke to a few people, who echoed the sentiments. The present and past CEOs and the chairpersons you have served under – they all hold you in very high esteem.

It is also evident that you enjoy considerable credibility and respect from your colleagues on the Group Executive Committee. They have expressed admiration for your patience, talents and insights. You bring balance and diversity of thought to the table. One of the comments

I heard goes as follows: 'With all the technocrats around her, she is measured and patient. She has a big heart. She is very intelligent, she takes everything in, reflects and offers a unique perspective, a diverse and pertinent view on very serious matters affecting the company and its people.' That is a powerful endorsement.

When your appointment to Sasol was announced in 2005, Pat Davies, the CEO at the time (who is with us here tonight), was quoted as follows:

'We are confident Nolitha will have a very positive impact in the portfolios for which she is responsible and that she will play a prominent and influential role in advancing our transformation ambitions at Sasol.'

Well, you certainly did make a positive impact, with dignity and grace. In my conversation with Pat, I was particularly struck by one of his comments when he said – and I quote – 'When you talk about changing a culture of the organisation, you cannot be insincere about something like that. You have to live it and epitomise it. And Nolitha was really good at helping us get that right.'

Nolitha, we are honoured by your humility, your empathy and kindness. It is this thoughtfulness that David Constable remembers, distinctly, when he first landed in South Africa to take on his new role as CEO of Sasol. He says you were the first one there, at his hotel, to welcome him and his family. You spent part of your weekend time helping them get settled. And as David and his family got to know you better, in and outside of the office, they were positively awed by your nature of 'inclusivity' and your respect for everyone, irrespective of their rank or station in life. That you are very approachable and you inspire people across the board is a theme that carried through all my conversations.

With your leadership style, your gravitas and yet, a quiet manner, some have described you as the glue that holds the place together. A recent *Financial Mail* article on Sasol identified you as 'Sasol's highly rated executive vice-president of Strategy and Sustainability', and I thought that was just fitting. The impact of your decisions and recommendations has positively affected the lives of many, like the unemployed graduates that you exposed to the Sasol operational environments, including Synfuels and Qatar, the Women's Mentorship Circle you started at Sasol and other initiatives. You have overseen the creation of a talented, dedicated and diverse workforce, which has been crucial to the success and image of Sasol over the last decade.

As I conclude, I would be remiss not to mention the role you have played in Sasol's external stakeholder relationships. Notably, you have been extremely helpful in getting the Sasol leadership to move forward with government relations. In fact, according to Hixonia, our former chairman, you somehow managed to be highly respected by many sectors of government without any kind of patronage. You certainly did not feel that you had to pander to them. So, with your consistent dignity inside and outside of Sasol, it could be said that you protected and enhanced the Sasol brand in many respects.

And so, tonight, after eleven years of a successful tenure with this great company, we recognise your immense contribution. As we pay tribute and bid you farewell, your generosity of spirit, your grace and the legacy you have created will leave an indelible mark on us as individuals, and the company as a whole.

On behalf of the board of directors of Sasol, the Group Executive Committee and the people of Sasol, we thank you, profoundly, for your valuable service, your leadership and your friendship.

PART 5

THE JOURNEY AHEAD

*We, the people of South Africa,
Recognise the injustices of our past;
Honour those who suffered for justice and freedom in our land;
Respect those who have worked to build and develop our country; and
Believe that South Africa belongs to all who live in it, united in our diversity.
We therefore, through our freely elected representatives, adopt this
Constitution as the supreme law of the Republic so as to*

❏ *Heal the divisions of the past and establish a society based on democratic values, social justice and fundamental human rights;*

❏ *Lay the foundations for a democratic and open society in which government is based on the will of the people and every citizen is equally protected by law;*

❏ *Improve the quality of life of all citizens and free the potential of each person; and*

❏ *Build a united and democratic South Africa able to take its rightful place as a sovereign state in the family of nations.*

*May God protect our people.
Nkosi Sikelel' iAfrika. Morena boloka setjhaba sa heso.
God seën Suid-Afrika. God bless South Africa.
Mudzimu fhatutshedza Afurika. Hosi katekisa Afrika.*

From the *Constitution of the Republic of South Africa, 1996 – Preamble*

CHAPTER 14

◇◇◇◇◇◇◇◇◇◇◇◇◇

Reigniting the gender agenda

It is now widely understood that a person can have multiple careers in a lifetime. David Constable's departure from Sasol presented an opportunity for me to reconsider my own path. Serving under two CEOs over eleven years at Sasol and having spent 26 years in the business world, I realised that, God willing, I may have another 25 years of active business life left. It was time for a gap year to re-energise and reflect on how to make the most of my second act. One thing that emerged very clearly for me in this time of contemplation was the urgency of putting gender equality back at the front and centre of transformation efforts. Recalling that one of my biggest conflicts in accepting the role at Sasol had been the necessity of stepping down from running for a second BMF presidency, my mind circled back to what had been left undone in a term of three rather than six years.

When I left the BMF presidency, two of nine BMF chairpersons were female and most branches had women in leadership positions. That said, we still fell short of the 30% target we had set to ensure that more women would emerge to take on national leadership roles. Our failure to continue adequately to fill the pipeline with qualified women is evidenced in the fact that nearly fifteen years later, I remain the only woman to have served as BMF president. This is a sore point for me, because I believe had we continued to drive the momentum around gender equality gained under my presidency, we would be seeing a lot more women leaders both within the BMF as well as other business structures today.

It was with this in mind that, having left Sasol, I realised I needed to dust off the various shoes I had journeyed in as BMF president all those years ago, re-lace my boots and recommit myself to promoting the gender agenda – it was time to join another dance.

The 'firstborn' generation: A responsibility and a privilege

Taking stock now, I feel that I perhaps could (and should) have pushed harder for the gender agenda even earlier in my career. Part of the blind spot came from the fact that in 1994, when as a country we first started talking about transformation, the most obvious pressing issue was racial inequality and the need for post-apartheid redress. For me and many others, what hit you back then was the whiteness of any given institution and the desire to see people who looked and talked like us, which, in that context, meant gravitating first and foremost to issues of South Africa's demographics.

As gender quickly became part of the transformation conversation, many private sector organisations attempted to get around employment equity or BEE targets by hiring white women to improve their numbers.[10] Those companies would say, 'Oh, we've got 50% gender diversity in our company; we just need to deal with the racial issue,' as if the latter were a cherry on top of their transformation efforts, which came down to five of their ten people being female, all of whom, it would turn out, were white. That strategy continues to reflect in the stats today, with white males still leading in management and leadership positions, followed by white females, then black males, and black females remaining at the bottom of the transformation ladder.

With the gender agenda partially hijacked by those trying to avoid dealing with the real issues of transformation and culture change, many of us – including black women – felt we had to keep our focus trained on racial discrimination. In this way, gender transformation and equality ended up undermined, and frankly the agenda has languished at all levels across all companies and types of engagements, and particularly across the racial divide.

Thinking back to the Carlton Centre conference in 1995, when we women were admonished by some of our black male colleagues to 'wait in the queue', it is with chagrin that I acknowledge how many still hold this view. To this day, you hear anecdotes and comments from black male colleagues and leaders that 'this gender equality thing' is going 'too fast', or that it's fine 'out there' but 'not in my house'. These kinds of comments are often said jokingly but in many instances much that is said in jest speaks to a deeper truth.

To be very clear: gender equality remains a problem for everyone, across all races. But the complexities that come with the racial divide – meaning the need to tackle gender *and* race simultaneously – make the problem even thornier. Which is why as much as I hesitate to open myself to misinterpretation, I feel the need to spark meaningful conversations around the gender agenda among and within the black community in particular.

Let me begin that conversation by focusing on one of the ways feminine power is recognised and upheld within African culture. In the Xhosa tradition, our firstborn daughters are called 'mafungwashe', which means 'the one you swear by'. Within families, mafungwashe is expected to act as a moral compass. She is the glue that binds the family together; hers is a highly influential role that acknowledges women's power. It is also a role that comes with a tremendous sense of responsibility, because you can be a mafungwashe who is very divisive within the family, or one who guides the family to harmony and prosperity. As a mafungwashe in my own family, the responsibility and privilege attached to this role were made particularly clear to me when I was about eighteen, and it was time for my younger brother Vuyo to go through ulwaluko, or his circumcision rite of passage.

The details of the ceremony are guarded closely by men, and women are not supposed to and do not feature. However, my mother wanted to ensure that my brother would be safe and properly looked after – a concern that would normally have fallen to our father, who was no longer there. Although my uncle was handling things, my mother, whose direct engagement in any part of the process would have been seen as disrespectful, wanted more assurance. Gathering my uncle and me a few days before the ceremony, my mother asked us to find out who the *ingcibi* (the surgeon) would be, and to speak with him. She wanted to make sure that he knew what he was doing, that he would do right by her son, and that – in so far as possible – he would see that my brother was first in line. (Normally there are five or ten boys being taken through the ceremony, and in those days sterilisation of tools was an even bigger issue that we, as women who didn't know exactly how things would happen, wanted to safeguard.) This is how I found myself joining my uncle to meet with the two men who would oversee this critical rite of passage in my brother's life.

My uncle organised the meeting, handling the introductions ahead of time so that when he and I arrived the two men knew I was there as mafungwashe, and therefore accepted my presence. In turn, I was able to reassure my mother who, the day before the ceremony, also had me go with my uncle to inspect the iboma (traditional hut) where my brother would be. 'You know how men are, he'll say it's fine when it's not fine,' she had worried. (For the record, I never saw or visited my brother on the night of his ulwaluko; I only visited him two weeks after his circumcision, as custom allowed, after umojiso.) While my mother's focus on my brother's safety and comfort in the ceremony that effectively initiated him as a man may seem excessive, underlying it was her desire that he not feel the absence of our father at this critical moment in his life as a man. That I was able to play the role I did, and be in those conversations because, as my uncle said, 'She's not just a girl, she's mafungwashe', was a balm to us all as a family. It also demonstrates one of the many ways in which African culture recognises and accommodates – even in that most sacred of male spaces – female power and responsibility.

That said, upon reflection, this story also illustrates for me the important role that economic independence plays in terms of a woman's ability – regardless of cultural context – to lay claim to her power. I did not see this at the time, but my mother's economic independence gave her leverage within our community, including with my uncles. It was only much later when I grew up and saw how other families and spaces worked, that I realised that even though we hadn't broken any cultural law, my presence had been possible both because our culture acknowledges women's important roles but also because my mother's position allowed us to fully claim the privileges of that role.

This brings me to another key point about privilege and being 'first'. Reflecting on my journey of 'firsts' in my career – first woman this, first black person that – I see a strong parallel between the privileges and responsibilities attached to being part of the generation of 'firstborns' in the boardroom, and those belonging to mafungwashe. That is, there are a lot of mafungwashes out there, not necessarily in the context I've just scoped, but by virtue of being firsts in different career spaces. And therefore I believe that if you are somewhere on a ticket of mafungwashe, there are expectations around you in terms of how you will use that opportunity and role to do good by those you represent, and rightfully so.

I know many women (and black people) are reluctant to accept such a role, insisting, 'But I'm here on merit.' And while that may be true, I believe you must also acknowledge that within that company or institution you are there representing your gender or race, whether you wish it or not. Personally, I am very clear on the fact that I would not be where I am today without affirmative action, and that South Africa's employment equity legislation was a factor in getting me into many boardrooms. Obviously, what I did with those opportunities once I got inside the boardrooms is all on me, for better or worse. My point is, I believe being a 'first' carries an extra responsibility and implied mandate to represent those who are not present, especially in environments that previously were populated exclusively by men.

Equal opportunity
Like all culture change, the gender agenda's reception is directly linked to where the broader external environment and culture is. Once again, we return to the issue of macrocosm and microcosm: that whatever is

happening in society plays itself back into organisations and business. It is no coincidence that when I became the first female president of the BMF, our country's president, Thabo Mbeki, was a gender activist of note, whose cabinet included at least 30% women, and that the general atmosphere was politically conducive to gender equality, with five of the nine provincial premiers also being female. Here we encounter an interesting dynamic that speaks to the relationship between leaders and culture: leaders guide the conversations we are having as well as create the culture that in turn influences who will be chosen as a leader.

This truth was displayed when President Mbeki stepped down. Across different sectors of our society, I saw the whole public narrative shift, with those who had not fully bought into gender equality emboldened to push the issue aside and drive other agendas. The gender agenda sadly was just one of many casualties in what became a large-scale and ongoing battle between transparency and fairness on one hand, and corruption and state capture on the other. The resulting environment, in which access to opportunity became increasingly unequal, not only stunted the promotion of gender equality, but also helped sexual harassment, among other ills, to thrive.

◇◇◇◇◇

Although it varies in levels of physical harm, I believe sexual harassment is a form of gender-based violence. On the 'lightest' level, it is that visceral surge that runs through your body when someone disregards your opinion, or responds with shock that you have something meaningful to say in a meeting on any given topic. There you are in a boardroom or meeting, and this person knows he can't chase you away, but doesn't know how to deal with you. Should he be formal or informal? Playful or not? Because he looks at you and sees someone to date, he lacks the tools in his psyche and socialisation to simply take you seriously as a colleague. The response is often to patronise or undermine you, which is a subtle form of harassment.

At the next level are the cases where colleagues in workplace settings behave inappropriately. In recent years, I have heard far too many stories from young black businesswomen who own companies concerning problems at this level. Entering into consortiums or the government 'tender space', they have found male counterparts treating them as if they are lucky to be there, and making it clear that sexual favours are expected in return for working together. My response has always been to point to our legislative frameworks (for example, the BEE, the EE, the Equality Act, and our Chapter 9 institutions), which give the woman in this scenario power and leverage. In other words, she should understand that her presence as a competent black businesswoman brings added value to any bid or company, and she must insist on being treated with respect and dignity. Fortunately, the last revised BBBEE codes and scorecard now acknowledge this; they include bonus points for women, especially African women.

But more women must speak up and bring these incidents into the open if we are to move forward. Usually the best place to start is with the other people involved in the deal or group, as this will help ensure your own protection against victimisation and prevent others from later claiming ignorance. Failing a positive response there, you escalate the situation, speaking to managers, union leaders, or even employing the confidential whistleblowing line that most private and public organisations have. You also must use the structures that are in place (for example, sexual harassment policies, which all companies should have) to prevent this kind of behaviour. Ultimately, however, your ability to insist on your rights begins with educating yourself and knowing what your rights are.

Unfortunately, due to the culture of unequal access to opportunity that I spoke of earlier, you will sometimes find that the person misbehaving has 'special connections' to the deal in question, causing others in the group to fear exclusion if they don't play along with whatever manner of illicit behaviour, and leaving you as the 'victim' with little recourse. In such a situation, the best advice I can give is to walk away with your dignity and integrity intact. Because while equal access to opportunity removes the middle person and these kinds of power dynamics, unequal access to opportunity has shown us how corruption at the top affects us in ways you would never have imagined.

The main difficulty in any of these situations is finding the courage to speak out. The ability to do this is often a function of how well the larger culture or environment truly supports transparency and equality. Even in private sector spaces, where women feel supported, these situations can remain largely muted because women fear that there will be some kind of economic retaliation. This speaks to the ways in which women's continued lack of economic empowerment and independence so often underlies gender-based violence – from the 'lightest' form of sexual harassment in the workplace to the devastating rates of domestic violence in our communities. I truly think that if women were more aware of their rights and had greater economic choices, they would be able to push back more forcefully against all of these situations. Which brings me back to the responsibility of leadership and organisations – from businesses to churches to schools to government – to create a culture and environment that actively promotes gender equality and nurtures and protects women.

And while the world of business needs to take these issues on more transparently, at the end of the day it is all of our responsibility to find more courage to do the right thing. This truth is recognised and supported by platforms such as the United Nations Women-initiated 'HeForShe' solidarity campaign for the advancement of gender equality. Grounded in the idea that gender inequality affects us all, it encourages men and women alike to accept a role as change agents, and to take action against negative stereotypes and behaviours. In other words, women and men need to support and mentor each other, as well as call each other out. In particular, men who want to live the values and principles of equality need to be more visible in terms of acting as role models. This means directly and indirectly mentoring and showing other men how a man in leadership should handle himself and behave. People literally need to see how it's done: how you treat women as equals, and how you engage in the basics of calling out your male peers if you see them behaving badly, especially when it is not obvious. At the end of the day, men who care about the gender agenda – and in particular, male leaders – need to say to each other, more often and more clearly: 'Not in my name.'

Fortunately, the context is always changing. I was reminded of this when, at the end of 2018 – less than a year into Cyril Ramaphosa's presidency – COSATU elected its first female president, causing me to wonder how much the external narrative in our country over the previous ten years had contributed to the delay in appointing women to senior positions in so many organisations. While it is still early days, I remain hopeful that a new champion around the gender agenda will emerge to bring us back from what must be acknowledged as a decade of regression vis-à-vis transformation.

Sharing the load

The general regression of the last decade notwithstanding, there have been improvements. Having served on boards of companies for virtually my whole career (beginning with being a branch chair at the BMF, then more formally being appointed to the Peoples Bank board in 1999, and currently sitting on a handful of JSE- and LSE-listed boards), I can say that board membership diversity in South Africa has improved significantly over the years. In fact, generally speaking, South African boards do better in terms of racial and gender diversity than many European and American companies.

That said, race and gender remain areas where boards – like all leadership spaces – continue to struggle to achieve anything close to equal representation. The lack of gender diversity on boards in particular has been highlighted in recent years, with calls for more women on boards sounded globally.[11] In spite of this encouraging recognition from boards and organisations about the importance of improved gender representation, my own vantage from various boardrooms shows me that we still have our work cut out for us in terms of the culture change needed to achieve gender equality both in South Africa and globally.

PART 5: THE JOURNEY AHEAD

The most fundamental issue remains ensuring that women get the opportunities they need to earn an income that will empower them to have more influence and choices. This goes back to understanding the basic issues that either grow or hinder the whole economy, which mostly come down to lack of opportunity to adequate education, training and development. A fundamental barrier to economic empowerment, especially for women, and inequality of opportunity is in part related to persistent and deep-rooted cultural perceptions that a woman's 'place' is not on top. Put another way, we are seen as liabilities in the workplace because of our potential to become mothers (and therefore having to take maternity leave). From girls whose parents only can afford to send one child to school and so choose their sons, to young women encouraged to pursue only certain careers, to teachers or bosses who dismiss female subordinates' potential, this cultural bias manifests in so many ways.

Despite all of this, girls and young women today continue to disprove gender stereotypes, and a wide range of global evidence shows that women's representation in higher education has actually increased to a rate equal to or exceeding men's. Yet while female representation in higher education and the junior levels of professions has improved so dramatically, it seems to falter and then practically disappear as you go up the professional ladder to higher levels of management and leadership. This reality is seen across the globe, and increasingly we are understanding that women's diminished presence 'at the top' is largely a result of the continued choice women are forced to make – by ourselves, by the culture, by the professional world – between family and career.

But certain countries – mainly in Scandinavia – demonstrate the possibility of an alternative where such choices do not have to be made. In Norway, where they have set targets for women's representation in various spheres of leadership, including boards, companies and society have together created an accommodating environment for women to thrive both in their careers and family lives. Policies that offer family or paternity leave in addition to maternity leave can act as levers that shift how childcare is approached, creating new norms around who does what within the home culture. It is this kind of ongoing societal commitment that needs to be made in more places, including South Africa.

Happily, in our South African context we are seeing more private sector support for early childhood development (ECD) care, but this cannot be left to companies alone. We need government-supported structures funding ECD and pre-school education so that it is a well-developed universal offering from which all women and families can benefit. Not only would this lead to better outcomes for our children, it unlocks the potential for women to return to work earlier and more easily, and thus continue to go further. Again, this goes back to cultural norms around how we conceptualise parenting as a society. As parenting and/or paternal leave (rather than just maternal leave) becomes more mainstream, families can choose who will spend time with children at which stage, and from a career perspective, the choice of having a family will cease to be something for which one is penalised. It is also worth considering the possibility that if men were better enabled (through better leave, societal acceptance, etc.) to take greater responsibility in child-rearing, the cultural and social value given to this function would also shift, and with it a whole slew of cultural baggage around gender norms, expectations and barriers could fall away.

Aligning the head and heart

So how do we get there? I think most people these days – black or white, male or female – accept and intellectually understand that we live in a constitutional democracy that says women and men are equal. Yet emotionally, too many retain the hang-ups and insecurities from their own life journeys that prevent them from embracing this intellectual knowledge in their hearts. In other words, the head and the heart remain disconnected. I believe connection comes through open and honest dialogue that allows people to acknowledge the challenges they are dealing with. Part of this is about calling things out for what they are. I think we may need to talk about this big word 'misogyny', and to do so in safe spaces where people can acknowledge how their socialisation and upbringing led to the emotional and cultural views they hold. As humans we need to have language to move through our challenges honestly and authentically, thus getting past them.

In other words, the gender agenda needs to be talked about. This means raising awareness that the current gender inequality is unacceptable, and acknowledging that the playing field still needs to be levelled so that women have equal access to opportunities, especially to training and leadership positions in all spheres of society. We need both women and men to champion gender equality, which must be understood not as a 'woman's' issue, but as central to better outcomes and prosperity for everyone. And all of this – demanding gender equality in all of its facets for all women – needs to be part of a greater national values-driven dialogue that should be taking place across all platforms from workplaces to religious institutions, political organisations and schools.

At its core, gender transformation is about a meaningful paradigm shift in the behaviour and mindsets and culture that are limiting us. As such, we must relentlessly ensure that the gender agenda is front and centre of everything we do. We need to stop talking about gender equality as something that is a 'good to have', but insist on becoming a society that is equal and fair and inclusive in the way that it engages with the entire population in all of its diversity.

CHAPTER 15

We need to talk

'We need to talk.' These four words can strike anxiety and fear in your heart, especially when said within the context of a relationship. It does not matter whether the relationship is romantic, friendly or professional – all you know is that the other person is indirectly telling you 'We are in trouble.' Immediately your mind races through various questions and scenarios: how big is the trouble? Who is to blame? Will it lead to a breakup, dismissal or even someone dying? That is how deeply those four words strike me.

In my view, we, the people of South Africa, urgently need to talk. Yes, *that* talk. After 25 years of democracy we must sit down and speak honestly about where we are on our transformation journey towards racial and gender equality. Looking back on my own path, from my childhood in Cenyu's general dealer store across South Africa's private sector to where I sit today, it is undeniable that as a country we have made massive strides. However, my story is far from the norm, and so much more could and should have been accomplished by now, especially in the private sector.

Taken on the whole, the private sector's transformation has had checkered results. On the positive, the numbers have in most instances improved. When you talk about targets, the demographics reflected in different sectors and industries continue to look better, with more black people and women acting in meaningful leadership roles at the hearts of businesses across our industries (though these numbers still need to grow). On the negative, there has been a muting of the meaningful qualitative conversations that must take place across the spectrum of society for real and deeper transformation to continue to take root and grow.

In the period from 1994 into the early 2000s, the level of discourse across boardrooms was vigorous and honest, and it felt like people were truly invested in understanding how to make workplaces embracing places for black people, women and those living with disabilities. Of course, the discrimination and prejudice then were more overt: you knew what you were dealing with and could name it clearly. Since that time, the pendulum has swung from a majority of private sector actors committed to achieving both the targets and the desired culture change to the majority going through the motions to get better BEE scores. Seen merely as another competitiveness tool, transformation compliance has become a tick-box habit, with few businesses using the BEE scorecard as a framework to help them drive and achieve genuine and sustainable culture change.

While such target chasing may continue to improve the numbers, it fails to address the cultural and value-driven problems that still underlie and drive the racism and sexism that are both symptoms and causes of a bigger system of inequality. Meanwhile, discrimination tends to be expressed in more sophisticated and covert ways, making it sometimes difficult even for the person who is on the receiving end to articulate what happened and how she knows it was prejudicial. This 'muting' of authentic dialogue around values and culture, and how we are doing things as a country, is preventing us from figuring out how to make the cake bigger so that all South Africans can have a meaningful slice.

The fact that so many South Africans are still barely managing is a situation that cannot be allowed to continue. Linked to the ways we are still floundering when it comes to the race and gender agendas, the economic inequality we see around us in South Africa has kept us fractured. In other words, having achieved political freedom, we still lack the economic emancipation that we need before we can be united as a nation. As indicated in the

Prelude, for us to experience peaceful co-existence among all South Africans of all races, deep and sustainable socio-economic transformation must take place. Anything less does not set us up for success as a country that is seeking a common shared future.

Recalling that moment in my girlhood when I was confronted by my mother's powerlessness against Jack and his vouchers, and how the whole economic game was rigged against us, I think about how many people today still feel they are living in that world of Jack's vouchers, even if Jack's colour has changed. Although the demographics of the haves have diversified, the fact that the majority of South Africans are still economically disempowered remains. As a result, if anything, there is less consensus around who we are as a nation today than in 1994. At the heart of that uncomfortable truth is the fact that our political freedom has not adequately changed our social and economic reality.

For all of these reasons, it is time to consolidate our thinking as a country. A quarter of a century into democracy, we need to take a step back and ask ourselves: who are we as South Africans, and who do we want to be? I believe we can arrive at an answer by engaging in a sincere and wide-reaching national dialogue. For us to achieve our full potential as a country, 'we need to talk'. It is my belief that sparking a national conversation could cause the pendulum to swing again, not back to where it was in 1994 but to a better and more evolved place than our forefathers and -mothers could have even imagined.

Such a dialogue would start by discussing the shared values we as South African society want to use to define what it means to be South African. Serving as an anchor or fixed point that we hold ourselves up to, wherever we are and however we operate, such values would also offer a gauge by which to measure our leaders. In rebasing our definitions of who we are as a people and country, and reassessing the values that will anchor that identity, our first point of departure would be our Constitution, the Preamble of which acknowledges our past inequalities in a manner that still makes me weep with gratitude when I read it.

My soapbox manifesto

So how do we start this talk? The conversations that we need to be having around our values and the continued transformation agenda – because the two are inextricably linked – require direction. We currently lack the containing force that leaders – and I include myself here – provide when they step up, take charge and say, 'Let's have this conversation as South Africans in a way that will help us to move forward.' Without this container and direction, our conversations around racism and sexism have felt uncontained and disconnected, hurtling towards some unknown precipice. This has been the case across all sectors of our society, from the workplace to schools to government. And while freefall does have its place in terms of process, so does leadership.

The main role of leadership is to positively direct the efforts and energy of the many forward. When leadership abdicates this responsibility, or adopts a narrative that is not in keeping with the values of its constituency – whether a company, organisation or whole country – the results are felt keenly. This is why I firmly believe that whatever the next step is in our transformation journey as a country, it needs to be the result of a positive public dialogue, directed and contained by leadership so as to break the freefall that we have been in.

While our Chapter 9 institutions would be clear collaborators in these conversations, leadership is not limited to big institutions or people who have run for political office or are presidents of anything. Leaders at all levels and from all platforms – from religious and faith-based institutions and schools, to companies of all sizes, civil society and government – can and must take charge of the dialogues and discussions around the work we still need to do to transform our culture and values in an honest and transparent way. Re-energising our national dialogue and returning our focus to the values that underlie nation-building, these leaders will become the much needed champions of this process. All change initiatives begin with a few core individuals, who champion change in different sectors, spheres and organisations, and become a movement because what they are saying resonates in others. In particular, we need to ensure that women and the youth are equally represented here.

Although I don't know what it will look like, I am sure that the role of the youth will be critical to this conversation. As such, I strongly believe that our best efforts must be made in schools, where we should begin the work of discussing shared values, common purpose and transformation from the earliest age, taking it through to the highest levels. After all, if these discussions are not taking place in school, where else are we hoping they will occur? And how do we expect young people to engage fully with the challenges of today and tomorrow if we have not adequately explained how we arrived at this point?

This brings to mind an incident that occurred last August when I was at a theatre production of *The Color Purple*. I was standing next to a group of young women outside the theatre, and overheard one of them asking what the holiday the next day – 9 August – was about. Here was this group of women in their 20s who, based on the context (at a production of one of the great works of one of the most acclaimed black feminist writers of our time) seemed very socially aware, and yet they were unable to connect Women's Day to the day in 1956 when a group of women marched to Pretoria to protest South Africa's pass laws. I was shocked to realise that this history is not more firmly embedded, either from conversations at home or school. Finding my best smile to crack into their conversation, I filled them in on the origins of the 'holiday'. They were pleased if slightly embarrassed by my unsolicited history lesson, and we exchanged details and have continued to engage.

The point is, the ability to discuss complex and difficult issues is a bit like language learning: fluency comes automatically with exposure if you are young enough. And this is important, because by the time young people get to the workplace, if they have gone through a school system that doesn't talk diversity and inclusion, so much is already lost. Engaging the youth also will bring parents into the mix. If you are exposed to new ideas because of what your kids bring home from school, and at the same time your workplace is educating you about these issues, it starts to build real momentum.

Finally, the youth will help to ensure that whatever form the national dialogue takes, it will cross-pollinate in parallel conversations on social media, which doubtless will serve as a key platform.

How do we get there: Rules of engagement

While I cannot predict what will come out of the conversations I am advocating for – by their nature they must not be prejudged – I do imagine that some dedicated organisational structure that can help bring different leaders together will be necessary to advance these nation-building conversations, the aim of which is to get to the next level of how to work through our gender, race, equality and diversity issues. Meanwhile, as a place to start, I have identified four 'rules of engagement' that I think could serve as a useful foundation:

> *First: Every voice counts*: All stakeholders must be around the table, all voices are equal, and everyone should be listened to. It goes back to Stephen Covey's principle, 'seek first to understand, then to be understood'. Seeking first to understand helps us to listen without judgement. It is only when we understand where someone else is coming from that we can fairly judge and decide how to engage. This requires sharpening one's listening skills, which is a particularly relevant aptitude in the era of social media. If our first response to any statement was 'What do you mean?' or 'Why are you saying that?' I believe we would have more reflective and thought-through responses, and less of the lashing out that we so often see these days. Personally, I would never have achieved the success I have, had I not made the effort to work *through* people. This meant focusing on the shared goal, shutting out the noise (especially when you can see someone is baiting you), biting your tongue, and finding the space to ask the other person, 'What do you really mean?' Besides, listening helps develop your ability to empathise, which is a core competence for future leaders.

Second: Do not lose sight of the goal: These conversations are about the future of our nation. We must keep focused on that vision, and not be side-tracked by red herrings. There are so many competing priorities that it is easy to lose our perspective as to why in the first instance we are having these conversations. Yes, we can spend time talking about *how* we got here; however, it is more important to focus on how we get out of this situation that we are in.

Third: Integrity and honesty are key: We have to be consistent with our truth and feelings, and not be persuaded by peer pressure and populism. Maintaining your integrity and being honest about how you feel or see things can be tough emotionally, and we therefore need to give each other feedback without emotion. With emotion comes accusation; with accusation comes defensiveness; and with defensiveness comes the inability to listen. When we don't listen to each other we start to shout, forgetting that we need to talk to find each other and find a way towards our common future. As they say, you have two ears and one mouth: use them in that ratio.

Fourth: No one is an island: We need to respect ourselves and others in order to live in harmony with each other. It goes back to 'Umuntu ngumuntu ngabantu' (I am because we are), the fundamental principle of ubuntu.

◇◇◇◇◇

I propose these rules of engagement merely as a starting point to spark a national conversation about values and transformation with as many people as possible. We must stop viewing transformation through the narrow lens that only sees decision-makers as capable of or responsible for driving change. All South Africans should be committed to understanding why the transformation and inclusion agendas are so important to our long-term success as a nation. Transformation is not only about righting the wrongs of the past; it is about creating a shared culture, identity and vision for us as South Africans through a truly consultative process. Despite being a key competence that more leaders should demonstrate, the consultative approach remains all too rare in business and politics alike.

During a radio interview after I had been appointed at Sasol, I was asked how I could be ready for such a big job. Reflecting on my different life experiences and exposures, I realised how they had all come together and finally made sense to me. It started with being raised by a mother who, for all her strength and independence, showed me the value of including people in discussions to reach consensus. I grew up being part of family discussions where we would discuss what needed to be done for the business, and in which my mother would share our plans and goals so we could all work together towards those things. From there, I spent time with and learned from the unions, learning how to negotiate with people and seek consensus to find a common ground on any issue. My work in change management then required me to guide multiple organisations to let go of past identities and structures in order to move forward to a shared future based on common values. Finally, my leadership experiences at the BMF consolidated a leadership style that was fundamentally based on a belief in influence over power. I also saw that part of my personal drive to be at the decision-making table was rooted in the fact that I hated not being consulted on matters that affect me, which I think has kept me sensitive to the need to communicate with people who are not part of the process.

⋄⋄⋄⋄⋄

Our transformation issues remain a key pressing problem, causing us to disintegrate as a nation and preventing the progress we could make if we were more unified. While we are fortunate in South Africa to have the legislative framework that provides us both the guidance and legal mechanisms to achieve transformation and equality, we are still journeying to arrive at that ideal place where targets and values coincide, and where the majority of our people can claim the economic emancipation that we had thought would come with political freedom. The reality that the two were not necessarily bound together has unfolded at a time when the world around us has become a place where the pressing issues of climate change, poverty and global political uncertainty ramp up. Added to those are South Africa's own big-ticket items – the economy, education and land reform. While prior to 1994 everyone wanted to help us, our young democracy has come of age, and in many respects we are now on our own to solve our problems, none of which can be handled well if we do not deal with our fundamental issues as a nation.

While the work of transformation is continuous and iterative, and numerous paths can take us in the right direction, one thing of which I am sure is that we will not arrive without an open and meaningful dialogue that can help us come to a shared understanding around our national values and identity. Different people will want to have the conversation for different reasons, but if we can find the common and shared values that anchor that interest, then we are halfway there. It is about recognising that what we want as humans is not so dissimilar. When you strip it down to the bare essentials, each person desires to live to their full potential, and to do that, certain things must be in place. Let's start that conversation – it's time for another dance.

APPENDIX

◇◇◇◇◇◇◇◇◇◇◇◇◇

Correspondence close to my heart

14 October 2003

Dear Nolitha

Congratulations to you, how wonderful, you must be so proud of yourself. I will never forget how you helped us with funding when you were at Woolworths. We no longer receive any funding from them.

Our school has grown from strength to strength with regards to our quality of training and graduate achievements.

Our first Graduate Andile Sotiya has his own company called Dancenomad and lives in the U.K. Our Second Mamela Nyamza is a freelance professional dancer living in Gauteng. Our third Songezo Mchilizeli is in his third and final year at the Pretoria Dance Technikon and on completion will be joining Tshwane Dance Company based in Gauteng.

Our fourth Graduate Mantu Jakavula is in his first year of a three-year National Ballet Diploma, he just recently received a Distinction

APPENDIX

98% for his Spanish Exam and in addition another Distinction for his External Royal Academy of Dance Classical Ballet Examination Intermediate level.

Keep in touch.

Kindest regards

ARLENE WESTERGAARD
PRINCIPAL
ZAMA DANCE SCHOOL

APPENDIX

12 November 2003

Dear Nolitha

Peri-hot Wishes

All of us in the world of flame-grilled peri-peri chicken would like to congratulate you on becoming the peri FIRST woman to be elected President of The Black Management Forum.

We wish you the best of cluck as you rule the roost at this professional and highly regarded organization. We at Nando's have full confidence that you will fill all 'five pairs of shoes', walk 'barefoot' peri-proudly and fly high!

In recognition of your HOT status and to help you celebrate your very feathery fine achievement, we're inviting you to tuck into some peri-peri chicken. We're delighted to enclose a complimentary Nando's voucher, with our warmest regards.

So when the craving speaks, only Nando's will satisfy. That's the time to strut into your nearest Nando's and use our spicy voucher for a complimentary meal. Get your claws into some mild, hot, or extra hot world-class chicken. Or be cool and peck away at our lemon and herb option.

May things go peri-ticularly well in your new role!

Peri-hot regards,
Kevin Utian
Managing Director
Nando's South Africa

APPENDIX

17 November 2005

Dear Mrs Njoli

I write to wish you and your family a wonderful weekend with Nolitha. We at Sasol feel very privileged to have her work with us.

As you know she is a special person. I believe she will make a huge difference to Sasol and, indeed, to our country. She is one of the only three executive directors (the youngest and prettiest as well!) of the largest South African domiciled company and has a very exciting and challenging career ahead of her. I assure you that we will give her all the support she needs.

Such a special person can only come from a very special mother and family — you have my admiration. On behalf of all of her friends at Sasol, I wish you a wonderful celebration. I hope to meet you in the future.

My very warm regards,
Pat Davies
Chief Executive
Sasol Ltd.

APPENDIX

[October 2006]

Nolitha

Thank you so much, dear, for the leadership skills, integrity, wisdom, mature behaviour that you have shown during your term. You are one in a million that has what it takes to do exploits in this country. A mark has been left in BMF by you in your era.

Many good things are coming up for you. The Lord has good plans not to harm but to prosper you. The Lord has engraved your name in the palm of his hand. As such no weapon that is formed for you would prosper.

Know one thing, that all things work together for good. There is a reason for everything. Even if wena akundazi mina kundala ndi ku bona and know one thing that there are people out there who are praying for you.

Keep well sisi
Lwando Bantom
BMF member
KZN annual conference

Abbreviations

ABASA	Advancement of Black Accountants of Southern Africa
ABSIP	Association of Black Securities and Investment Professionals
AFCON	Africa Cup of Nations
AMEF	African Minerals and Energy Forum
ANC	African National Congress
ANCWL	ANC Women's League
ANCYL	ANC Youth League
ASGISA	Accelerated and Skills Growth Initiative for South Africa
BBBEE	Broad-Based Black Economic Empowerment
BBC	Black Business Council
BEE	Black Economic Empowerment
BITF	Black Information Technology Forum
BLA	Black Lawyers Association
BLSA	Business Leadership South Africa
BMF	Black Management Forum
BoE	Board of Executors
BPF	Black Professionals Forum
BSA	Business South Africa
BUSA	Business Unity South Africa
CEPPWAWU	Chemical, Energy, Paper, Printing, Wood and Allied Workers' Union

ABBREVIATIONS

CHIETA	Chemical Industries Education and Training Authority
CODESA	Convention for a Democratic South Africa
COSATU	Congress of South African Trade Unions
CSR	corporate social responsibility
ECD	early childhood development
EE	Employment Equity
EPC	engineering, procurement and construction
FABCOS	Foundation for African Business and Consumer Services
FSC	Financial Services Charter
FTSE	Financial Times Stock Exchange 100 Index
GIBS	Gordon Institute of Business Science
HRDC	Human Resource Development Council
ICT	Information and communications technology
IEC	Independent Electoral Commission
JSE	Johannesburg Stock Exchange
LSE	London Stock Exchange
MD	Managing Director
MP	Member of Parliament
NAFCOC	National African Federated Chamber of Commerce
NBBC	National Black Business Caucus
NBS	Natal Building Society
NDP	National Development Plan
NEDLAC	National Economic Development and Labour Council
NGP	New Growth Plan
NQF	National Qualifications Framework
NUM	National Union of Mineworkers
RDP	Reconstruction and Development Programme
SABC	South African Broadcasting Corporation
SACCAWU	South African Commercial, Catering and Allied Workers Union
SEP	Senior Executive Programme
SETA	Sector Education and Training Authority

ABBREVIATIONS

TRC	Truth and Reconciliation Commission
UNITRA	University of Transkei
WBF	Women's Business Forum
WEF	World Economic Forum

Notes

1 Other major black associations include NAFCOC (National African Federated Chamber of Commerce and Industry), the BLA (Black Lawyers Association), ABASA (Advancement of Black Accountants of Southern Africa), BITF (Black Information Technology Forum), and the BBC (Black Business Council).
2 South Africa's 'transformation laws' refers to: Skills Development Act 97 of 1998; Employment Equity Act 55 of 1998; and the Broad-Based Black Economic Empowerment Act 53 of 2003, known as the BEE Act.
3 Now going by Mzwanele Manyi; we called him Jimmy Manyi at the time.
4 The Skills Development Act 97 of 1998, the Employment Equity Act 55 of 1998, and the Broad-Based Black Economic Empowerment Act 53 of 2003, known as the BEE Act. Although the BEE Act was not passed into law until 2003, the BEE Commission, which was established after the BMF's 1997 conference, actively debated and discussed what that act would include during the period under discussion here.
5 The Congress of South African Trade Unions is a trade union federation in South Africa. Founded in 1985, it is the largest of the country's three main trade union federations, with 21 affiliated trade unions.
6 The skills levy is paid in taxes. Some companies commit more to skills development on top of this, usually somewhere between 2–5% of the wage salary.
7 South Africa's key economic policy from 2005–2010, the Accelerated and Shared Growth Initiative for South Africa (ASGISA) envisioned the aims of reducing poverty by 2010 and halving unemployment by 2014 by putting policies to address these issues at the forefront of economic policy decision-making. Building on the foundations of the RDP's goals of building a united, democratic, non-sexist and non-racial society, and

a single integrated economy, ASGISA was replaced in 2010 by Jacob Zuma's New Growth Plan, which in turn gave way in 2013 to the National Development Plan. (SOURCE: https://www.sahistory.org.za/article/south-africa%E2%80%99s-key-economic-policies-changes-1994-2013).

8 Defined in 1998 under the Skills Development Act, the SETA, or Sector Education and Training Authority, is the country's vocational skills and training system, whose goal was to develop a series of sector skills plans within a clearly defined framework of the National Skills Development Strategy. Concerned with education and training across South Africa's major economic sectors and industries, each SETA is responsible for managing and creating learnerships, internships, unit-based skills programmes and apprenticeships within its jurisdiction. Every industry and occupation in South Africa is covered by one of the 21 SETAs. (SOURCE: https://seta-southafrica.com).

9 SOURCE: https://www.iol.co.za/news/south-africa/sa-skills-shortage-an-urban-legend-354132.

10 The EE and BEE targets for gender did not specify race. Thus a company's improved gender diversity would score points on the BEE scorecard even if they did not include a single black person, male or female.

11 Although initiatives like the '30% club' have helped increase female representation on FTSE-100 boards from 12.5% to 28.9%, we need many more of these kinds of efforts.

Acknowledgements

Lee Middleton, my collaborator and writing coach: thank you for reintroducing me to the art of storytelling.

To my Njoli family, especially my siblings, Vuyo (Bra V.), Siyolo (Bhutana) and Vuyelwa (Mavuyi): thank you for meeting me halfway, especially in loving our larger than life mother – uNoDumo, iBhelekazi, the love of my life …

George Suliali, my partner: thanks for the anchoring friendship and love. You're my 'Atlas Man' – you make the journey easier. Your boundless support while writing this book ensured that I completed the project with the same energy that I started it with.

Thanks to Lee and George, who had to contend with my 'moments' of mini meltdowns during some tough reflection sessions. There is indeed an art in being a great listener. Thank you both for listening and editing.

My colleagues from Woolies, BMF, Nedbank and Sasol – you know who you are! If I were to mention all of you by name, I would need a whole chapter just for that. Your graciousness towards me, often when I did not even believe in my own ability to carry on, the many hours when each of you gave

ACKNOWLEDGEMENTS

me an ear or a chance to exhale or a shoulder to cry on – for this I am forever grateful. I count you all as my blessings. Over the years, as the song goes, all of you were the wind beneath my wings. I'm deeply touched that our paths crossed. For what I owe you and even if I pay it all forward in double measure, it still will not be enough.

The Pan Macmillan team have been great collaborators with me on this project. Without Terry Morris's guidance and Sibongile Machika's excitement at the idea of a business book that was not only just a business book but a memoir, I would have found the last mile daunting. Thank you for your moral support.

With Andrea Nattrass and Alison Lowry's firm and knowledgeable guidance and editing, the manuscript evolved into a book as if by magic, with less drama than I had anticipated. Thank you team Pan Macmillan for your nurturing support.

Thank you to all the BMF members, past and present, for raising this young girl into an adult. You are all my chosen family come rain or shine.

My deepest gratitude goes to Dr Phumzile Mlambo-Ngcuka, who not only wrote the Foreword to this memoir, but has been a consistent role model and champion to many South Africans of my generation. Your generosity of spirit inspires me all the time.

Dr Reuel Khoza, Wendy Luhabe and Futhi Mtoba, thank you for honouring me with your thoughtful messages, which have added great weight to this memoir. Your taking the time to give your context and perspective to my journey has further deepened my resolve to continue being part of the dance, whatever steps might be required going forward.

Lastly, to fellow South Africans, thank you for allowing me to dance ...

Selected references and suggested reading

Arnold, M.W. (Ed.). (2017). *The Testimony of Steve Biko*. Picador Africa: Johannesburg.
Barrett, R. (1998). *Liberating the Corporate Soul: Building a Visionary Organization*. Butterworth-Heinemann: Oxford.
The Black Management Forum (BMF). (2014). *About Us*. Available from: https://bmfonline.co.za/index.php/leadership (accessed on 26 July 2019).
Covey, S.R. (2013). *The 7 Habits of Highly Effective People: Powerful Lessons in Personal Change*. Simon and Schuster: New York.
The Department of Trade and Industry (DTI). (2013). 'A Bold New Trajectory for B-BBEE'. In *The National Broad-Based Black Economic Empowerment Summit*. Available from: http://www.dti.gov.za/economic_empowerment/docs/National_Summit_Report.pdf (accessed on 26 July 2019).
Estès, C.P. (1996). *Women who Run with the Wolves: Myths and Stories of the Wild Woman Archetype*. Ballantine Books: New York.
Houston, W. and Winans, C. (1995). *Count on Me*. Arista Records: New York.
The Human Resource Development Council of South Africa (HRDC). (2010). *Who We Are*. Available from: http://hrdcsa.org.za/who-we-are/ (accessed on 26 July 2019).
Khosa, R.J. (2005). *Let Africa Lead: African Transformational Leadership for 21st Century Business*. Vezubuntu Publishing: Johannesburg.
Molefi, N. (2017). *A Journey of Diversity and Inclusion in South Africa: Guidelines for Leading Inclusively*. KR Publishing: Johannesburg.
Mutwa, V.C. (2001). *Indaba, My Children: African Tribal History, Legends, Customs and Religious Beliefs*. Canongate Books: Edinburgh.
Nedbank. (n.d.). *Equity Investors*. Available from: https://www.nedbank.co.za/content/nedbank/desktop/gt/en/investor-relations/investor-center/share-price-information-.html (accessed on 26 July 2019).

SELECTED REFERENCES AND SUGGESTED READING

Oriah Mountain Dreamer. (2006). *The Invitation.* HarperCollins: New York.

Quinn, R.E. (2004). *Building the Bridge as You Walk On It: A Guide for Leading Change.* Jossey-Bass: San Francisco.

Sasol. (2001). *JSE Listing.* Available from: https://www.sasol.com/investor-centre/share-and-dividend-information/jse-listing (accessed on 26 July 2019).

South African Government. (1996). Preamble. In *The Constitution of the Republic of South Africa.* Department of Justice: Pretoria.

The South African Institute of Chartered Accountants (SAICA). (2015). *Employment Equity Act, No 55 of 1998.* Available from: https://www.saica.co.za/Technical/LegalandGovernance/Legislation/EmploymentEquityActNo55of1998/tabid/3041/language/en-ZA/Default.aspx (accessed on 26 July 2019).

United Nations. (2015). *Sustainable Development Goals.* Available from: https://sustainabledevelopment.un.org/?menu=1300 (accessed on 26 July 2019).

Woolworths Holdings Limited. (2017). *Investors.* Available from: https://www.woolworthsholdings.co.za/investors/sens/ (accessed on 26 July 2019).